Beyond
Angels and Demons

Beyond
Angels and Demons

The Truth Behind the Fiction

René Chandelle

CHARTWELL
BOOKS, INC.

CONTENTS

INTRODUCTION

INTRODUCTION

Are we being subjected to a worldwide conspiracy? Who controls the media? Are there seemingly innocent, but fanatical powers that dominate society? Who is interested in secret societies? Do they really exist? How far does their sphere of influence reach?

Conspiracy is not a new phenomenon. Nor are the initiation ceremonies linked to secret societies. It is a morbid, curious subject, shrouded in mystery, which makes it even more attractive, but...where is the reality?

The Da Vinci Code exposed some grim secrets. It opened a door, showing a glimpse of certain conspiracies, jealously guarded throughout the centuries. Dan Brown, the book's author, aired these forbidden ideas with the delicacy of a Vatican librarian and with the agility of Ian Fleming. The subject is not a new one. Furthermore, decades before, some investigators had already proposed different hypotheses on the life of Jesus. Nevertheless, it has forced us to see and be aware of things that have been astutely ignored, or by chance perhaps have gone unnoticed.

The new code, formulated by a sequence of numbers, phrases, facts and images, when properly linked together, offers a new message and the discovery of new secrets. In this instance, it is not the hidden life of Jesus. In *Angels and Demons*, other issues are raised, perhaps even more dangerous, corrosive and at the same time, more terrifying: an open war against the power of the Church, led by a group called the Illuminati.

The reader who opens Dan Brown's book, like all those who devoured *The Da Vinci Code*, crosses the threshold of reality and enters a universe of secrecy. To read *Angels and Demons* is to cross a tangible line and witness incredible plots, propagated by the hatred of this secret society. The main theme of this work is a new form of terrorism, the spiritual kind. This cannot be analysed from a literary context, but only from a more realistic one, one with far more impact than the novel.

Following the September 11 attacks, one phrase had more validity than ever: 'reality always transcends fiction'. How much of *Angels and Demons* is true? How much can be believed? No one doubts the existence of the Vatican, Bernini's masterpieces or the temples that, while being very real, are like a set in a work of fiction. Galileo is not a character invented by a film director. Nevertheless, other surprising aspects of the book may send a shiver down the spine when the undercurrent of reality they possess is registered. A glance is all it takes to realise that fiction is an open book capable of casting light on a reality known by few.

In the 11th century Hasan ibn Sabbah founded a sect inspired by a fanatical and radical branch of Ismailism: the Assassins or *Hash-ashin*, meaning those who consume hashish. They killed their victims with tremendous cruelty, because of their euphoric drug-induced state. In the 13th century more than 12,000 members of this group were condemned to death. Many managed to escape, dispersing quietly to Syria....Where are their descendents today?

In 1776, Adam Weishaupt created the sect – the Iluminati of Bavaria. His goal was to steer the human being onto the correct path of pure spirituality. The way to do this was to eradicate governments and private ownership, dissolve monarchies and install authoritarian republics. Although the dates are vague, it appears that the order was dissolved in 1785, at least in the eyes of the public... But this is no more than the beginning of the story.

Ambigrams (words or phrases written so that they can be read the right way up or upside down) do not come from Dan Brown's new book. Their remote origin is in magic books, designed to be read and interpreted only by learned masters. In reality, thousands of people in the world 'play' with these ideas, assuming them simply to be word games, part of the mystical and magical past and no more than an amusing pastime.

The reader will be able to verify that the references included so far are no more than inklings of reality that many will be able to find in *Angels and Demons*. But there are other aspects that we cannot overlook. These have to do with the other terminologies that allude to the Masons, the Rosicrucians and those who are linked to the secret worldwide conspiracy through acronyms and names that, if nothing else, are thought-provoking. For example, the OSS (Office of Strategic Studies), the name of the investigative group that was the precursor to the CIA, and the Masonic Lodge Propaganda 2 (P2), one of the most powerful groups in Italy.

By now thousands of people have read *Angels and Demons*, and a seed of doubt has been planted in their minds: does the possibility of a spiritual terrorist attack exist? We believe so. Nevertheless, the entire affair extends further. In fact, one only has to think of the attacks on the Twin Towers, the war in Afghanistan, the war in Iraq or the Palestine–Israeli conflict, as a reminder that something is ocurring.

We live in a new world order. This is a phrase popularized by the father of the current president of the United States, during the first Gulf War, and, as can be seen, it has a certain link to the Illuminati: those who are called 'Novos Ordo Seculorum'.

The question is: who runs this new order? Perhaps the answer is:

governments in the shadows, who in turn might be directed by those controlled by this movement, those who are a part of this determined secret society. But there still remains another question to resolve: where will all this lead us?

The reality behind the work of Dan Brown, which will be analysed objectively in the following chapters, is much more subtle, but it is also very revealing and worrying. The conspiracy is now underway. Our subject begins to unwind.

PART 1

THE
WORLDWIDE
CONSPIRACY OF
SECRET
SOCIETIES

1. Beyond Angels and Demons

'We say that two types of poetic mind exist: one able to invent fables and another disposed to believe them.'
Galileo Galilei.

To find out about the secret messages hidden in *Angels and Demons* requires us to travel back in time by a few centuries. This way, it is easier to understand Galileo's thoughts and the nature of scientific life in his lifetime; what his colleagues and patrons thought and believed and, most importantly, who influenced his ideas. The exciting story of this extraordinary mind best symbolizes the point of rupture between science and the Church. It was a historical moment when knowledge and dogma took different paths, and science was driven into the dark.

THE ASTRONOMER FROM PISA

Galileo Galilei was born in Pisa in 1564. Ten years later his father, the musician Vincenzo Galilei, moved the family to Florence. Galileo studied at a monastery close to the city, and later entered the Faculty of Medicine at the University of Pisa. It is said that one day the young 16-year-old student observed a hanging lamp swinging in the cathedral. He figured that to complete an oscillation the same length of time needed to elapse to cover the same distance. This discovery later enabled him to elaborate on the principle of the pendulum, which he would apply, amongst other uses, to regulate the movement of watches. From that day Galileo was interested more in exact sciences than in medicine, to the extent that he abandoned the latter to begin studying astronomy and physics in Tuscany and Florence. After leaving university, he published an essay on hydrostatic balance that became known throughout Italy. In the following years he dedicated himself to revising the

Nicolas Copernicus, anonymous portrait of the astronomer. The first scientist to successfully formulate and demonstrate the possibility of the heliocentric system.

Aristotelian theory of movement, and in 1592 he obtained the professorship of mathematics at the University of Padua. He stayed there for 18 years and completed his own theory of movement and of the parabolic path of projectiles. No one knows if it is true that he tested his hypothesis by dropping weights from the Leaning Tower of Pisa, but it is true that his other passion, astronomy, started to create problems for him with the Church.

Galileo was an adherent of the hypothesis of the heliocentric universe, formulated two centuries earlier by Copernicus, which can be summed up as the idea that the Sun does not orbit around the Earth, as Ptolemy had demonstrated in the 2nd century. Ptolemy's argument was adopted as official science from then on – despite the truth being exactly the opposite. Galileo did not make his opinion public, in order not to incur the scorn of his colleagues and because he was wary and suspicious of the Church's reaction. But in 1609 he tried out a simple telescope and he became fascinated with the contraption. In the same year he built a telescope 32 times more powerful, and used it for the first time to look at the heavens. The following year he made known his first discoveries about the Moon, the phases of Venus and the satellites of Jupiter.

SCIENCE ON TRIAL

The Vatican, starting to become suspicious of some of the more dissident scientists who had turned away from the Scriptures' teachings, celebrated the works of Galileo and various dignitaries of the papal court showed a sincere interest in the telescope. Naïvely encouraged by their approval, Galileo published some observations on the Sun in 1613 that upheld Copernicus theory. Enraged Dominican priests proclaimed that this mathematical heresy contradicted the cosmogenical version of Genesis. Although they did not mention Galileo by name in the pulpit, they secretly cited him before the Inquisition.

Frightened by this denunciation, Galileo turned to close friends, in person and in letter, from the Grand Duke of Tuscany to one of his students who was a Benedictine monk. He argued, in a way unheard of at the time, that the Bible was an allegorical text, that its earthly rendition was open to any number of interpretations. Several ecclesiastical experts agreed with him, but not Cardinal Roberto Bellarmino, the supreme arbiter for the Church in all theological matters. The prelate roundly vetoed the idea that the mathematical hypothesis was related to physical reality. No one knows if this was because he did not really believe it himself or because he did not want to ignite a theological scandal that would weaken the Holy See during its tough fight with Protestantism. So, to put an end to the subject, he officially declared the Copernican theory 'false and absurd' and ordered the works of the genial Polish astronomer to be included in the Index (books banned by the Vatican). A few days before he published these decisions, Bellarmino met with Galileo in his office in the Vatican. The ruthless Cardinal advised his unhappy visitor on the measures he should take, warning him not to uphold or defend anything that the Church or Bellarmino himself had declared ungodly. However, with respect to Galileo's inspiring interest for science, he allowed him to continue to discuss with his colleagues and study Copernicus' doctrine in private, as a simple 'mathematical speculation'. Galileo withdrew to his house near Florence to continue his scientific investigations. There he coined his famous phrase 'the book on Nature was written with mathematical characters', in a work dedicated to his friend and protector, Cardinal Maffeo Barberini, who had just been elected Pope as Urban VIII.

Confident in his old friendship with the new Pope, Galileo presented himself in Rome in 1624, in the hope that the 'Bellarmino Decree' might be repealed, so that he would be able to publish his final works. This did not happen, but the Pope allowed him to write a book on 'the systems of the world', which could include the Copernican heliocentric model as long as it covered Ptolemy's geocentric idea as well. Galileo even thought that Urban suggested the idea to him that 'Man does not have to pretend how the world was made, because creation is a mystery of divine omnipotence'.

The rift between science and the Church had begun, and Galileo knew on which side he should fight. In 1632 he published his great work, *Dialogue on the Two Chief Systems of the World – Ptolemaic and Copernican*. No doubt, the title complied with the Pope's suggestion, but the content was an incendiary and undeniable defence of Copernicus theory. It produced admiration and enthusiasm in scientific spheres

The old friendship between Galileo and Pope Urban VIII and the obtained imprimature (an official approval from the Roman Catholic Church stating that a literary or similar work is totally free from error in all matters of faith and doctrine and hence acceptable reading for faithful Catholics) did not manage to prevent his trial by the Holy Office.

throughout Europe, but not in the ecclesiastical circles of Rome, where it immediately drew criticism. The Jesuits, for example, believed that Galileo had done more harm to the Roman Church than the Lutherans and Calvinists combined. Urban VIII, angry with his old friend, ordered the start of a trial. The distracted censors had approved the book, probably becauseof the arrest of one of reader, and this was the main reason for their failure to include it in the *Index*. But the Pope disapproved of the '*nihil obstat*' and completely prohibited the printing and distribution of Galileo's work. It appears that, in the meeting with Bellarmino in 1616, Galileo had promised not to 'teach or discuss Copernicanism in any sense', on penalty of being charged by the Holy Office.

The tribunal met and was authorized to initiate a trial of alleged heresy. Despite his 70 years and his frailty, the astronomer was obliged to travel to Rome in February 1633, to attend the court. Galileo argued that he did not remember the promise made before Bellarmino, perhaps blaming his advanced age. The judges appeared kind and indulgent, and when they were disposed to let him go with only a reprimand, a decree appeared from the congregation of the Inquisition that said he had to be sentenced. The verdict insisted that he 'forswear, curse and detest' his past errors regarding his sacrilegious ideas on the movement of the Earth. The crestfallen scientist uttered that abhorrent oath, and the story goes that upon leaving he murmured, '*eppur si muove*' (and yet it moves), insisting on his spectacular discovery.

Galileo continued to work and made important discoveries and contributions to science until his death in 1642. Apart from his unquestionable status as a scientist, the personal punishment he suffered for defending objective and rational thought made him an icon of scientific freedom.

THE SCIENTISTS AND THE SECRET SOCIETIES

Galileo was a standard-bearer of his time, but he was not alone. Perhaps submission to judicial proceedings, which led to his subsequent retraction of his theories, is what he is remembered for. But the astronomer of Pisa was not the only one. Around him, and practising the same and other disciplines, were many scientists who did not always rely on the approval of the established power, which at that time was the Church. In Galileo's time, to investigate science meant to depend on rich and powerful patrons, who in turn were 'guided' or directed by the Church. Patrons were unable to support theories that did not square up to the established canon. This stirred something that had long been lying dormant. Something that would

The Trial

Below are sections of the trial of alleged heresy invoked by the Holy Office against Galileo Galilei:

The Condemnation

'We say, pronounce, sentence and declare, that you, Galileo Galilei, have presented yourself, with accordance of this Holy Office, vehemently suspected of heresy, having held and believed a doctrine which is false and contrary to the Holy Scriptures, for believing that the Sun is the centre of the universe and does not move from east to west and for holding and defending this opinion, even after it has been declared and defined as contrary to the Holy Scriptures.

We, in this Holy Office, considering your absolution with a first condition which is, your retraction in our presence, with a sincere heart and with true faith, of these cursed and detested aforementioned errors and the heresies, and any other error or heresy contrary to the Catholic and Apostolic Roman Church. Only in this manner will we be able to absolve you.'

The Retraction

Galileo, under pressure and threats of the inquisitors, finally opted to retract the theories he had defended up until then:

'I, Galileo Galilei, son of Vincenzio Galilei of Florence, aged 70 years, swear that I have always believed, believe now and with God's help, will believe in the future, all that the Holy Roman and Apostolic Church holds, preaches and teaches.

After having been admonished by this Holy Office, I entirely abandon the false opinion that the Sun is the centre of the Universe and is an unmoveable body, and that the Earth is not the centre of the same and that it moves. I accept that I cannot have, defend or teach in any manner, with written or spoken, all that has been proclaimed a false belief.

Nevertheless, wishing to remove from the minds of your Eminences and all faithful Christians, this vehement suspicion reasonably conceived against me, I abjure with authentic faith and a sincere heart that I curse and detest the said errors and heresies, and also any other error, heresy or sect contrary to the Holy Catholic Church. I swear that for the future I will neither say nor assert in speaking or writing such things as may bring upon me similar suspicion, and if I know any heretic, or one suspected of heresy, I will denounce him to this Holy Office, or to the Inquisitor and Ordinary of the place in which I may be.'

linger for a long time… The conspiracy theory or, if preferred, the formation of secret societies.

In spite of the absolute domination of the Church, scientists knew that other forms of thought existed, as did other ways of understanding life and the magnitude of these things. They firmly believed that methodology was not always dictated by religious dogma. They had to ignore the Church and, logically, continue in secret. At that time numerous groups existed that sought protection in other philosophies, in esoterics and of course, in the occult ideas of distant oriental religions and whoever gave funding and money to new ideas. The secret societies supported the scientific advances and so science went under cover.

The moment arrived when the secret societies had not only proliferated, but also grown in membership. Their objective was clear: to face up to established power, liberating those who had always been told what and when to believe. At the time, this meant opposing the Church and its dogmas. In many cases it was not just a question of defending a scientific theory, but a way of life, of society and also politics. The conspirators, or those who did not conform to the earthly ecclesiastical power, should have united to act as a single force. But the truth is that the conspirators and their methods for advancing their schemes were manifold. And when we talk of secret societies we need to bear in mind this wealth of variety.

As time went on, the secret societies began to exercise a greater influence. They participated in major historical episodes, like the French Revolution, the American War of Independence and, more recently, in the two world wars of the 20th century, not to mention other more recent events. The question is where will it all end? The author of *Angels and Demons* offers us some clues on the matter, but we should not get ahead of ourselves. Like all good plots, the exact details of certain moments and exact circumstances have not been revealed yet, and this may take centuries to come about.

THE SECRET ADVENTURE OF FREE THOUGHT

During the 16th century there was a change in science and all its forms and philosophies. A new scientific method was born; one which was more modern and more experimental. And the investigators started to question things that until that time seemed unquestionable. The usual laws of science were beginning to crumble; the established laws started to break down.

A new scientific society emerged, and it started to question the established powers' beliefs, especially those of the ecclesiastical hierarchies. It was true that the investigators had to maintain a certain discretion, and at times absolute secrecy, to carry out their discoveries without arousing the wrath of the Church. We have seen Galileo suffer the pains of prison, condemned to retract his heretical theories. The Aragonese doctor and theologian Miguel Servet, who was accused of heresy for questioning the dogma of the Trinity, was condemned to die at the stake, while other scientists and notable thinkers were persecuted or died in strange circumstances. The Vatican and the 'learned' who received their money and their prebends were disposed to stop the new knowledge destroying their power by whatever means necessary. But the scientists carried on, often protected in secrecy, because they believed in the sentiment expressed by the great Galileo in this paragraph:

Miguel Servet, Aragonese doctor and theologian, argued in one of his works that the soul resided in the blood – the reason he was condemned to die at the stake for heresy.

Science is written in the biggest of all the books, the universe, which is permanently open before our eyes, but it cannot be understood without learning to understand its language and the characters with which it is written. It is written in mathematical language and the characters are triangles, circles and other geometric figures, without these it is humanly impossible to understand one single word, leaving a vague infuriating path through an obscure labyrinth....

Scientists in Galileo's time defended the necessity to study new ideas, to observe new phenomena and to experiment. Naturally such things are never simple and the new science was slow to take off and well removed from the established law. All the investigators and discoverers of that time documented their speculations and theories in private, at their meetings, but not through the official doctrine.

The Italian universities of the Renaissance were the most prestigious and appreciative of the donations made by their ostentatious patrons. To investigate and work somewhere other than Padua, Pisa, Bologne or Pavia was to run the risk of falling into anonymity. These universities were so modern, that the science of that time was spoken in Italian or Latin, the 'pure languages' that governed the lines of communications between the scientific societies. They taught the thoughts of the most renowned scientists in their cloisters and offered them the best patronage for their investigations. Of course a subsidy was required for the risks taken and for refuge if the clergy considered they had gone too far.

It is true that not all the European universities reacted favourably to the changes. The University of Salamanca, for example, which at other

These are some of the more meaningful advances that emerged during the new scientific era:

1. Mathematics
- A complete change in the study of classical algebra, which dated back to ancient Egypt and Babylon.
- A more modern algebra started in the 16th century by Niccolo Fontana, better known as Tartaglia (1500–1557), one of the discoverers of the ways to solve cubic equations.
- Mathematical science started to be applied to dynamics and physics, thanks to Galileo, as well as to celestial mechanics and optics.

2. Optics
- Significant advances were made that revolutionized previous knowledge. The first lenses were created, which consequently led to the first microscopes.
- In 1609 Galileo (1564–1642) made his telescope famous for being able to observe sunspots and the mountains of the moon, as well as the four major satellites of Jupiter and the phases of Venus.
- The rules of geometric optics started to expand.

3. Medicine
- New theories began to take hold. The anatomist and doctor William Harvey (1578–1657) discovered blood circulation while another doctor, Miguel de Servet (1511–1553), further described secondary blood circulation.
- Important discoveries were made regarding the heart as the organ responsible for blood circulation.
- Studies on microscopic anatomy were advanced.

times was a focal point for anatomical and astronomical investigations, preferred to be prudent throughout this period of scientific change. Its staff did not accept the new theories, and took refuge in the classic traditions that were accepted and protected by the Church. It was a similar case at the Sorbonne, where any new scientific theories were not accepted for fear that to do so would create problems in the theology to which they adhered. On the other hand, the University of Montpellier welcomed the winds of change with open arms.

THE MEN WHO CHANGED THE WORLD

We cannot judge the historical coherence of Dan Brown's novel; we must realize that the licence fiction offers allowed him to write mischievously about historical themes where necessary. We do not know if Galileo actually said 'when I look in the telescope at the planets, I hear the voice of God in the music of the spheres'; what we do know is that Pythagoras (585–500 BC) who celebrated philosophy and Greek mathematics, coined the phrase 'music of the spheres'. More precisely, after Aristotle, Pythagoras said on one occasion: 'There is geometry in the humming of the cords, there is music in the space that separates the spheres'.

Returning now to those determined, clear-thinking minds of the time of Galileo. Can one be sure that some of them felt obliged to meet in secret? It is very probable that this was so. It is acknowledged that some of these scientists established links with secret associations of the time. Although compared with the groups that had become true lodges, they were probably actually small splinter groups that met up to discuss and theorize about the new times. And even though the then big names of science were not Illuminati members, given that this sect did not yet exist, without a doubt they became close to the secret societies or sympathized with them, because they represented a possible protection against ecclesiastical intolerance.

Between 1609 and 1610 Galileo Galilei made the first observations of the Moon with his telescope.

The Illustrious Minds

Without a doubt the investigators and European scholars adhered to the possibility of a new more free, rational and independent science for hundreds, or even thousands, of years. Below are the most significant proponents, whose works were giant leaps in the advances of human knowledge.

• **Nicholas Copernicus 1473–1543** – Astronomer. He theorized that the planets orbited the Sun. Remember that until the advent of this theory, science was ruled by the postulations of Ptolemy, who claimed that the Earth was the centre of the universe, circled by the rest of the celestial bodies.

• **Francis Bacon 1561–1626** – Philosopher and politician. One of the most outstanding thinkers of the time, a true and valiant defender of a new vision of the world. Unlike many others, he did not just say what he thought, but he also wrote it down.

• **Galileo Galilei 1564–1642** – Mathematician, physicist and astronomer. Iconic exponent of the new science, he formulated important thoughts in the three disciplines. His work revolutionized the way the world and the universe are seen, thanks to his first telescopic observations of the stars, confirming Copernicus's theories.

• **Johannes Kepler 1571–1630** – Astronomer. His investigations concluded that the planets' orbits were elliptical. He discovered that the Sun generated a force on the other celestial bodies that was inversely proportional to the planets it drove.

• **Blaise Pascal 1623–1662** Philosopher and mathematician. Pascal's Principle that states that liquid transmits equal pressure in all directions. His conclusion that, 'human progress will be assessed by the accumulation of scientific discoveries' caused anxiety within the Church.

• **Isaac Newton 1642–1727** Mathematician and physicist. His exceptional contribution was the discovery of universal gravity, which affects all bodies. But most outstanding, from an esoteric and conspiratorial point of view, was his interest in alchemy. He also stressed his studies on mysticism. He believed in the ability to reach the elevation of intelligence by looking for direct contact with God, therefore going beyond the Church.

THE ENIGMA OF FRANCIS BACON

Before devoting himself entirely to study and to philosophy, the noteworthy English thinker, Francis Bacon, had reached high political and diplomatic positions, as well as obtaining the titles Viscount of St Albans and Baron Verulam for his services to the Crown. In 1618, when he held the prestigious title of Lord Chancellor, he was embroiled in a confusing lawsuit for bribery that put an end to his political career. It is not improbable that his fall actually corresponded to a conspiracy to destroy someone who was in turn a conspirator, a member of a powerful secret lodge.

At 18 years of age, after the death of his father, the young Bacon entered Gray's Inn, one of the Inns of Court in London where lawyers train to become barristers. In 1582 he obtained a licence to practise law and embarked upon his legal and political career, which took him to Parliament in 1600. Three years later, the ascent of James I gave new impetus to the political ambitions of Francis Bacon. He climbed ever higher in his career, until he was made Lord Chancellor in 1618, acquiring the title of baron, and two years later, viscount.

Suddenly, at the peak of his career, he was detained, accused of abusing his position by favouring certain people who had bribed him. The trial found him guilty of bribery, but the King converted his sentence, although advising him to leave public life. Sir Francis, who had already written some paragraphs of the *Novum Organum*, in which he proposed a new scientific method, listened to the royal advice. He dedicated the rest of his life to writing an extensive series of treatises and books on diverse subjects that brought him fame as a philosopher and admiration as a writer. But he never revealed the secrets of the trial or the mysterious acts that led to it. Enthusiastic defender of the modern scientific methods, Bacon published various articles and pamphlets, promoting a naturalistic and experimental focus. In one of these, he expanded on his scientific collections saying:

There have only been three great societies in history, Greece, Rome and Europe, in which science has progressed. Nevertheless, hesitation still reigns. We need to use the inquiry into nature as a method of investigation. We need to give an outlet to the spirit of man and allow him to experiment beyond the borders imposed by the usual criteria. We need to fight to feel that there is more than what we have accepted until today.

Francis Bacon, English philosopher, politician and writer, was connected with various secret societies.

Some 'conspiratorial' authors wanted to see Bacon as a member of one of the secret societies of the time. They offer as proof, as mentioned, that the case of bribery that brought about his fall was a ploy used by Vatican agents, and that he wrote two works of philosophy which delighted Adam Weishaupt, creator of the Illuminati of Bavaria. One of these was the *Treatise on the Value and Progress of Science*, in 1605, where he brilliantly defended the rigour and independence of scientists. The other, *New Atlantis*, published after his death in 1626, is openly esoteric from the very first page. Bacon describes in it a utopian and perfect world, organized like a universal democratic republic, where mysticism and science exist together in total harmony. Doubtless this was a deliberate reference to the lost era before the Flood, which all secret societies worthy of the term wanted to regain.

It is true that there is evidence that Bacon was connected with various sects of an esoteric character. There has also been speculation regarding possible contacts he had with the followers of an ancestral cult with philosophical and spiritual leanings, which had the thought-provoking name 'Rosicrucian'.

AN AGE-OLD SECT

In *Angels and Demons*, when it says there is an Illuminati link to the scientists of Galileo's age that gathered in the Church of Illuminati, nothing leads us to think of the Rosicrucians. Curiously there is a fact that relates the reality to the fiction in the book we are dealing with. The Rosicrucians really existed and, unlike the Illuminati, they were interested in science. Apart from Brown's novelistic fiction, the reality is that in Galileo's era some scientists gathered in secret. There is proof of some of these meetings around 1614, but the attendees could not have been Illuminati members, because the sect had not yet been founded.

The majority of secret societies claimed to originate from glorious epochs in a distant past. So, if we believe the supposedly ancient archives of the Rosicrucians, we have to go back to the time of the Pharaoh Tutmosis III, between 1504 and 1447 BC. In that era, numerous secretive schools existed, made up of scholars, priests, magicians and seers. Apparently, on the day he celebrated his coronation as pharaoh, Tutmosis had a revelation. According to Rosicrucian archives, he explained he felt lifted up to the heavens and later, after seeing a powerful light, received the instruction to bring together mystical knowledge. He then decided to create a secretive organization that he named the 'Great White Brotherhood', and instituted a code that would govern all its members.

Seventy years later, Amenhotep IV, who as pharaoh was the supreme Pontiff of the Brotherhood, reached new levels of wisdom and spiritual enlightenment. He changed his name to Akhenaten in reference to his devotion to a single god, Aten, represented by the Sun. Together with his wife, Nefertiti,

The Invisible School of the Rosicrucians, according to an illustration by Theophilus Schweighardt, in *Speculum sophicum rhodo-stauroticum*, 1618.

he established the first monotheistic cult and promoted a new spiritual and artistic culture of humanistic inspiration. It is of interest that there is no doubt that Moses, who features in the three largest monotheistic creeds of today, was a practising member of the cult of Aten.

When Akhenaten died, the traditional priests atempted to reinstate the lost religion, through their domination over the weak Tutankhamen. It was a dark time for the White Brotherhood, which would later be revived thanks to the Greek philosopher Thales of Mileto and the mathematician Pythagoras through their supposed participation in the Order. Both were responsible for spreading the teachings of the ancient Rosicrucians to Greek culture. Much later, this corresponded with the mission of Pliny of Alexandria who, in 244, founded a school of philosophy in Rome based in part on the secret teachings of the Great White Brotherhood. However, not until the 17th century did the word Rosicrucian appear as the new name of this hermetic society. In 1610 a book was published in Germany by an anonymous author who said he had compiled a document based on the writings he had discovered six years earlier in a tomb. The tomb was that of Christian Rosenkreutz.

This work told us of the life of a man educated in medicine, science, mathematics and the magic arts, as well as alchemy and physics. A scholar who had investigated the history of the occult in Egypt, a country

Bass-relief in limestone, representing Akhenaton and Nerfertiti with their children (c. 1345 BC). Akhenaton established a monotheistic cult akin to the Rosicrucian society.

where he had access to the esoteric texts attributed to Thoth, the moon god, and the inventor of the script adopted by the Greeks under another of his names – Hermes Trimegistus. It is believed that in Egypt, Rosenkreutz was initiated into the sect and was taught by the secret masters of the ancient Great White Brotherhood. He was then given, or gave himself, the mission to spread the Order to the rest of the world.

THE STRANGE MR ROSENKREUTZ

In 1378, in a less than noble family of German country folk, a child was born. Later he would adopt the name Christian Rosenkreutz, which translates literally from the German for 'Christian of the Pink Cross', and whose symbolic connotations are evident. His parents entrusted his upbringing and education to a monastery, where he learnt Latin, Greek, theology and the rudiments of the science of the time.

According to the modern biography written by the Rosicrucian brother Petros Xristos, the young Rosenkreutz took an 'arduous and risky' first pilgrimage with a fellow student to the Holy Land. No one knows if his companion died or they simply became separated in Cyprus, but it is certain that Christian continued to travel alone from this point on. He stayed in various places in the region, including Damascus, before finally arriving in Jerusalem. He stayed in the Temple for a long time where, according to Petrus Christus, he heard echoes of the message of the prophets and the teachings of Jesus.

Close to Jerusalem there was another temple, belonging to a secret esoteric order whose name, *Damkar* (Blood of the Lamb), alluded to the sacrifice at Calvary. The biography says that there the young outsider passed the initiation ceremony and took the allegorical name of Christian Rosenkreutz. But Christus pointed out that other authors believe that Rosenkreutz was in fact the founder of an order, a precursor to the Rosicrucians, who wished to return the secret of the true evangelical message to the Holy Land. In order to spread his esoteric knowledge, Christian learned Hebrew and Arabic, and succeeded in translating into Latin at least one hermitic book, probably gnostic or arcane in origin, which he then carried with him on his return to Europe.

He later went on the trip to Egypt that would mark his destiny, and travelled to various places around the Mediterranean, visiting and founding headquarters of esoteric societies, after which he spent some time in Fez, in Morocco, to learn Kabbalah and spread his knowledge of mysticism. From there, having already become one of the great experts in hermetic wisdom, he began a journey to Spain. On his route across the

A supposed portrait of Christian Rosenkreutz, founder of the enigmatic brotherhood of the Rosenkreuzer.

Iberian peninsula, he struck up a friendship with some monks, with whom he could probably share his knowledge, and created at the time something akin to a branch of the White Brotherhood: the Brothers of the Rosicruz. Subsequently its members were known as 'Rosenkreuzer', which gave rise to the false idea that it referred to a separate sect.

The mysterious Christian Rosenkreutz died, supposedly, in 1484 at the incredible age of 106. He took all his knowledge to his grave and there was an inscription upon his tombstone that read: 'He will reappear after 120 years'. And it really was so, given that the date of the discovery of his writings corresponds with this prediction.

In the wake of that discovery, a large number of English and German Rosicrucians moved to America as colonists, trying to establish new brotherhoods and spread their knowledge in the British colonies of the New World. They printed books, organized study groups and established contact with other colonies that had descended from lodges like the

The Six Basic Rules of the Rosicrucians

In the book *Fama Franternitatis* it is revealed that the first Rosicrucians complied with the following rules:
• Heal whomever necessary, using all available medical knowledge, without charging money for your services.
• Maintain anonymity wherever you go, suppress your own habits and always follow the customs of where you are.
• Meet once a year in the Temple to swap knowledge, and in doing so renew the links of the brotherhood.
• Each member must be responsible for perpetuating the mission of the Order, in order to initiate a successor before they die.
• Adopt the initials RC (Rosenkreuzer) as a password and symbol of the Order.
• Always keep the existence of the brotherhood secret.

Masons, and perhaps like the Illuminati as well. Their hard work resulted in Masonic leaders like Benjamin Franklin and Thomas Jefferson who also belonged to the Rosicrucian societies.

DOES THE ROSICRUCIAN CONSPIRACY EXIST?

At this point in time, the Rosicrucians have more than 300,000 followers in the world, with lodges in every continent. It is not a secret society as one would normally think of it; however, without a doubt, in the beginning it did operate with some secrecy. The important thing about the Rosicrucians was their love for science, for spiritual investigation and esotericism. Apparently, they were linked to people such as Da Vinci, Paracelsus, Newton and Cagliostro. The last appears in the history of conspiracies of the 18th century, as active within Masonic circles.

One needs to understand that the followers of Rosicrucian philosophy did not exactly agree with many of the scientific parameters and philosophies promoted by the Church. They maintained that religion, despite preaching the existence of the soul and its permanence in what lies beyond, was lost in conjecture and contradictions when it claimed dominion over the spiritual dimensions of man. The Rosicrucians preferred to believe in reincarnation. They thought it necessary to complete different grades of experience and acquire levels of wisdom that could only be

Robert Fludd's
Rosenkreuzer image,
Summom Bonum, 1626.

learned through successive lives. Obviously, this idea did not accord with the doctrine of the Church.

Another aspect of the Rosicrucians was their search for internal enlightenment. This meant the need to find happiness in life, and that development was supposedly carried out by living pleasantly in the material and spiritual world. They affirmed that their essential aim was to encourage human beings to realize the power of the mind, apply it in the right way, and become capable of dominating the teachings. They preached that the process of apprenticeship allowed them to manage the large atavistic mysteries, the eminent thoughts that they were conscious of, and to look for and understand the invisible. It was first necessary to analyse the visible. Obviously none of these concepts conformed with those of the orthodoxy of the day.

INITIATION AND HIERARCHIES OF THE ROSICRUCIANS

In general, the Rosicrucians were an open order, although there was a certain amount of secrecy. Rosicrucian brothers were entrusted with selecting those who would be their pupils, without any religious, social or economic discrimination. The candidate had to pass the so-called 'phase of preparation', first reaching the level of 'postulate' and later that of 'neophyte'. After these two initial stages came another three that he moved up through as he gained more knowledge. Then, the aspiring member passed on to a further period of study in order to qualify as an 'initiated' member. Afterwards, he had to pass to other new levels called 'Temple Grades'. Progression through these higher grades required successful completion of, amongst other courses:
• Study of the laws governing microcosms and macrocosms.
• Study of the laws governing the function of the conscience and its development.
• Study of the laws of life with the aim of understanding where we come from, where we are and where we are going.
• Study of the principal works of ancient Greek philosophy.
• Anatomical study of the human body as well as the principles governing health and creating illness, particularly of the internal and external symptoms they bring about.
• Analysis and study of all and each of the functions of the body, both the physical and the mental.
• Investigation and comprehension of the global and personal human soul in order to understand the existing links between them and the reason of their existence in the earthly plain.

Reception rite of those who reached the level of Master; certain Rosicrucian rites and ceremonies were adopted or inspired by other secret societies.

• Study of the hermetic and esoteric sciences, including symbolism, alchemy, kabbalah, divinination, mental powers and contact with other planes of reality, as well as all those works that have served as points of reference for the Order along the centuries.

By passing the above courses, the initiated person would attain the nine grades of the Temple, converting to Illumination and entering a new phase of teaching, to reach three further grades unknown to us.

It is doubtful that the Rosicrucians were linked with the geopolitical conspiracies to which other secret societies are devoted. The Order, through the centuries, has dedicated itself to the study of the functions of the human body, the principles that govern both health and illness, the intrinsic workings of the planet and nature, the formation of the universal soul and other studies that can be directly or indirectly related to the quest for God. The Rosicrucians saw themselves as a balance, as a point of conceptual and philosophical support to other secret societies. They really did appear this way, and it is possible that a good part of the rituals, ceremonies or esoteric practices of some of the above-mentioned secret societies were inspired or directly adopted from the Rosicrucians.

THE ALUMBRADOS: THE ESOTERIC CONSPIRACY IN SPAIN

The Alumbrados were a mystical and esoteric sect in the 16th century. They were founded in Castile, although other investigators say the sect was also formed in Andalusia and Estremadura. Wherever their place of birth, they attempted to reproduce the primal idea of the secret society of the Illuminati, formed in the mountains of Afghanistan at the same time (see page 46). These Illuminati sought to attain human perfection by achieving great magic powers though secret rituals. They intended to use this magical influence to change the attitudes of the political leaders of their time, with the goal of establishing worldwide harmony.

The Alumbrados also wanted to reach a state of physical, mental and spiritual perfection, using transcendental prayer as a medium. They put aside their good works and sacred practices ordained by the Church. The Alumbrados considered that, thanks to mental disciplines, including both fasting and sensory isolation, they could enter into contact with the Holy Spirit. However, they were considered laymen and only understood the Holy Spirit as a simple symbol, capable of awakening in them psychic powers and dormant spiritual meanings. They also believed that secret messages existed in the Bible and that rather than being just a sacred or religious book, it could actually be a path strewn with cryptic signs to be solved in order to achieve enlightenment.

The Alumbrado movement emerged under the shadow of Franciscan doctrine, which, like other ecclesiastical institutions saw themselves as intermediaries in individual relationships with God and impeded a more profound personal religious experience. In this era, immediately after the Expulsion of the Moors from Spain, an eagerness for mysticism, revelations and manifestations of a spiritual nature was widespread in Spain, as was a hunger for the preachings of the Alumbrados. It was the era of contemplative nuns falling into ecstasy, of anchorites, apparitions and visions. It was influenced by the idea of an 'internal religion' advocated by Erasmus of Rotterdam, in contrast to formal religion, and to be encouraged by a passion for mysticism. The Holy See, having tolerated these ideas at the beginning, finally decided to intervene.

Although the first Inquisitorial conviction of the Alumbrados was made in 1525, it was not until 1620 that the Inquisition achieved the almost complete eradication of followers of this doctrine. It is believed that some members of the sect decided to seek exile in France, where they were called 'Les Illuminés'. They separated from the main group, and established themselves in France 140 years before the appearance of the Illuminati of Avignon (see page 46), so they were well placed later to exercise influence over this group.

Accused of heresy, the Alumbrados were condemned by the Inquisition on 23 September in 1525 because the Holy See saw a link between them and Protestant spirituality. Nevertheless and despite the condemnation, their ideas inspired other minds that carried on further, beyond the Church's tentacles.

THE LODGE OF THE FUTURE

As we have seen, the 16th and 17th centuries were rich in learning, not just in the arts and the sciences, but also in the quest for wisdom through other methods not recognized by the established powers of the Church. At that time, plots against the Vatican seemed to be the order of the day, but the intrigue had only just begun. Control would be taken by a primitive Freemasonry, which was to be the real protagonist over the next few centuries.

A new Masonry that would patiently await the birth of a secret society of excellence – this is to what *Angels and Demons* refers: the Illuminati. A group that that would how to be inspired by those who had gone before them and would have the ability to take shelter in the heart of the Masons in order to carry through their mission to the end.

2. The Masonic Conspiracy

New Friends, new pains.
Mozart

Few see how we are, but all see how we appear to be.
Machiavelli

In *Angels and Demons* we saw that those who seek wisdom and who in the book appear to be Illuminati are exterminated. But in secret societies, nothing dies out, everything changes. In the book it explains how the Illuminati were able to survive:

The Illuminati were survivors (...) They were given refuge by another secret society, a brotherhood of rich stonemasons (...) The Masons fell victim to their own benevolence. After harbouring the fleeing scientists in the 1700s, the Masons unknowingly became a front for the Illuminati. The Illuminati grew within their ranks, gradually taking over positions of power within the lodges (...) Then the Illuminati used the worldwide connection of Masonic lodges to spread their influence.

How much truth is in this passage from the book? Freemasonry was initially an esoteric and secret society, whose origin goes back to the religious brotherhoods of the union of the English and French Masons in the 12th and 13th centuries. Nevertheless, this simple form of Masonry is not the same, as we have already said, as the one created in 1717 (or at least the group that was founded in this year).

THE DISPUTED ORIGIN OF THE MASONS

The esoteric, cultural and ritual affinities of Masonry go back to the mysteries of the Greeks and Egyptians. This secret society links Pythagorean natural philosophy to Neoplatonism, passing through Kabbalah, Celtic and Druidic traditions, as well as Arabic, Hebrew and Oriental esoteric thought. In addition to the participation of the stonemasons in the construction of impressive Gothic cathedrals, the legend says that the Masonic builders also participated directly in the construction of Temple of Jerusalem, which was devised by Solomon, the wise king who sought a connection with the divine.

Beyond the possible link between the Masons and Solomon and the construction of his Temple, it is probable that the Masons, both stonecutters and sculptors, had a significant involvement in the construction of the Gothic cathedrals. In these they included significant secret symbols, and as well as creating a temple whose final completion was a tribute to God, everything seems to indicate that they were capable of 'building temples inside temples'. In this way, they constructed of cathedrals with their own their esoteric sanctuaries contained within them.

The typical rose windows, clear examples of Gothic art, were not just windows that allowed light to pass through. The stained glass and the figures filtering the splendour of the sunlight inspired meditation, introspection and the connection with the divine.

A cathedral's gargoyles, which decorate the gutters while diverting the rainwater, were in principle archetypes that alluded to moral and spiritual values. It is true that demonic images can be found amongst the gargoyles, but this according to tradition, indicated that evil should remain outside of the sacred building. But there also were figures in embarrassing or pornographic poses. Were these a diversion for the artisans or a surreptitious attack on the morals and dignity of the Church?

A deeper look into the construction of Gothic cathedrals is not appropriate here as they are not the subject of this book. For those interested in knowing more we recommend the Fulcanelli's controversial work, *The Mystery of the Cathedrals*, which contains some surprising ideas.

The Masons' other great legend is the building of the temple of Solomon in Jerusalem, which contains the Ark of the Covenant.

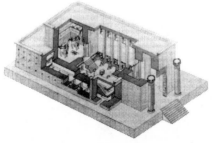

Artist's impression of the Temple of Solomon; according to legend, Masonic architects directly participated in the construction of this, the most sacred temple in Hebrew tradition.

The Temple of Solomon

Solomon was the ancient king of Israel, who governed between the years 961 and 922 BC. He was the second son of David, founder of the Judea and the Batsheba dynasty. In both Hebrew and Muslim traditions, King Solomon is considered a special person, capable of establishing connections with the invisible world and dealing with the spiritual entities that had links with divine planes.

The great work of Solomon was the Temple of Jerusalem, built over a period of seven years, with as much splendour as the age permitted. It was not likely that the Masons were involved in the building, although the chronicles speak of an enclosure full of magical symbolism and special energies that allowed sensitive and spiritually elevated people to reach modified states of conscience or if you prefer, the connection with the divine.

The Temple was a sanctuary with a door dominated by two hollow bronze columns nearly ten metres high and two metres in diameter. The enclosure was built for the Ark of the Covenant, which was guarded by two wooden cherubs covered in gold engravings. For the Jews, the Ark was actually a sacred container that held the rod of Aaron, a bowl of manna and the tablets of the Ten Commandments that Moses received on Mount Sinai.

CONTRADICTIONS IN MASONRY TODAY

Whether or not they came from the times of Solomon, via the medieval cathedrals, the tangible presence of Masonry is registered very solidly in historic legends. It is known that in 1717 the Great Lodge of England emerged, while in 1732 the Great Lodge of France appeared. Presumably both followed a specific moral system that was expressed through allegory and symbols. Nevertheless, beyond this nature, about which we can only speculate, the emergence and growth of Masonry in history has more to do with a secret relationship with politics and conspiracies than with a simple search for the supreme mystical-spiritual truth.

The form of Freemasonry that came into existence in the 18th century, was now no longer associated with stonemasons who tried to teach the profession to all, under the roof of a united lodge. Now the members were people of higher social status, endowed with both an interest in and influence on political and religious circles. The Masons had a motto, which some decades later was became associated with the French Revolution: 'Liberty, equality, fraternity', and the name of the lodge in English is 'Freemasonry'. Nevertheless it must be pointed out that there was little or no inclusiveness about the English Masons. Firstly, people of black origin were totally excluded. It was considered that they were an inferior race and could therefore not participate in the mission, which was to build the metaphorical cathedral, not just for the Church but also for man, both in this life and the after.

English Masonry did not allow women in their ranks. In fact, the social fight for the rights of women did not start until 1851, and even today, women remain excluded, as are people of African origin. On the other hand, a large degree of permissiveness existed in French Masonry, since they welcomed religious, political and sexual diversity. The Lodge established in France was of Scottish origin, springing from the House of Stuart, which was considered the guardian of the tradition of the French temples and which, 400 years before the foundation of the Masonry, had participated in the Scottish conquest. The English Lodges were organized following the York Rite (which also became the name of the American lodge), which was based on ranks, or Masonic grades. The French opted for something rather like the 'Old and Accepted Scottish' rite composed of 33 grades. In fact, this Scottish rite would influence the majority in the European continent and America.

The expansion of Masonry was much discussed and notorious, to the extent that in 1738 Pope Clement XII published a papal bull condemning the Masons and attempting to exclude them from the Church. A few years later Pope Benedict XIV would endorse this view. This exclusion has been maintained until the present day: Pope John Paul II included the Masons in a document on banned

A French Mason shown with the regalia from the lodge, from the 18th century.

organizations given to the Congregation for the Propagation of the Faith in 1983.

It seemed that, more than the Illuminati, those who really 'bothered' the Church were the Masons. Of course, with condemnations like those mentioned above, and those that continued coming, especially from the pen of Pope John Paul II, one must ask if it is a conflict that for centuries the Masons have maintained with the Church, or rather, vice versa.

Despite this hostility, at the beginning of the second half of the 18th century the Masons continued with almost all of their activities. However, the French Revolution provoked a crisis that lessened and even

The Masons had a motto, which a few decades later was used by the French Revolution: 'Liberty, equality, fraternity'.

caused some Lodges to shut down. However, by coming through this period, many Lodges became stronger still and have lasted to the present day. Nowadays, it is calculated that there are approximately 5,000,000 Masons in the world. While in the beginning there were two rites, today an infinite number exist spawned from the ten grades of the York Rite and the 90 of the Misraim Rite.

DOES A MASONIC CONSPIRACY EXIST?

If we know what the Masonic precepts are based upon, and understand their origins and how they are organized, then the suspicion that some Illuminati members infiltrated their ranks in the 18th century does not seem strange. While the Masons appeared entirely innocent and wanted the creation of a more enlightened Universe, the Illuminati wanted social and political, rather than mystical, power, and found in Freemasonry the perfect front to achieve their objectives. Nonetheless, the aim of the Masons was not as innocent as it may at first appear.

The Masons were the main protagonists of the Enlightenment, and so influenced the French Revolution; they were heavily involved in the independence and foundation of the United States and, in the 20th century, were players in both world wars, as well other events or world importance.

It cannot fail to appear to be a paradox that a mystical society, with a policy of keeping politics outside the temple, had so much involvement in politics in history. Possibly this was the real Masonic conspiracy.

IN SEARCH OF A WORLD GOVERNMENT

One of the many conspiracy theories about secret sects linked to the Rosicrucians and the Knights Templar was their alleged quest for a world government. Everything seems to indicate that it was the Masons who adopted the idea and altered certain of their stated objectives. History states that after the death of the last Templar Grand Master, his followers had precise instructions to perpetuate the Order, to create an invisible secret society, to integrate into already existing groups or to create new and hidden groups: called 'invisibles'.

The story goes that a small group of remaining Templars founded the Order of St Andrew of the Royal Thistle, later named the Invisible School.

As well as scholars, the above Order had a number of scientists among its members whose aim was to promote science and distance themselves from the patronage imposed on them by the clergy. In the middle of the 17th century, the Invisible School became the Royal Society, which today still appears to have close links to the Rosicrucians and the Masons.

Among the members of the Invisible School was a man of uncertain origin and mysterious demeanour called Comenius. His idea was the creation of a 'pansofia', that is, a universal doctrine capable of governing the world. Some of his proposals were:

• The creation of a World Parliament.
• Universal reform of society in general.
• Reform of religious, political and philosophical concepts.
• The creation of a Supreme Tribunal whose mission would be to watch over the reconciliation of religions, at the end of which the entire planet would be peacefully consecrated with God.
• The establishment of an International Court of Justice capable of mediating the world's political conflicts.
• The establishment of a world council of learned men, called The Superior Unknown, with a mission of eradicating, ignorance, atheism and any inkling of social regression.

As we have seen, the complexity of their plot – which had to remain completely secret – was remarkable. The question is: did they achieve their goals? What are they doing now? It is at all possible to suspect that many of their objectives have actually been achieved?

3. The Conspiracy of Bavaria

*The truth is not the language of the court; it only emerges on the lips
of those who distrust or fear somebody else's power.*

Giuseppe Mazzini

In the novel *Angels and Demons*, after the death through poisoning of one
Pope, members of the secret society of the Illuminati prepare to fulfil their
sinister plan to destroy the Catholic Church, taking advantage of the
conclave gathered to choose a new Pope. They are the main conspirators
who, with the help of a member of the Arabic sect of the Assassins, hatch
plans to destabilize the church hierarchy, and at the same time, as the
ultimate coup de grâce, literally blow up the Vatican using an antimatter
bomb.

This is the essence of the plot of Dan Brown's novel, which has
been taken as the subject of this present study. There are elements in this
work based in reality, but also bordering on fiction; for example the
mention of the bomb. Other elements, such as Pope John Paul I, who died
33 days into his reign and may have known of a secret conspiracy, are more
likely. There are also some other conveniently manipulated elements,
which the author takes from traditions and texts about secret societies and
other esoteric fountains.

The Illuminati are mentioned right at the beginning of the novel.
They make their entrance in a scene with an attractive ambigram (a text
that is read from left to right, and which appears the same after being
rotated through 180 degrees), a symbolic and cryptic writing technique.
However, it is not clear if ambigrams were actually used by the real
Illuminati. Another interesting aspect in this work of fiction is that the
creation of the Illuminati is said to be in the time of Galileo, giving the
impression that the scientists in those days had to meet in secret to
exchange their investigations far away from the pressure exerted upon them
by the Church. It is sad to disillusion the reader, but there is no proof that
Galileo or Copernicus, to name the two greatest astronomers, were
Illuminati members, especially given that the secret society did not exist at
that time, at least not officially, even though there were other sects that
might have adopted dissident investigators.

In this section the questions requiring answers are: When did the
Illuminati really come into being? Who was behind the group? What was
their secret objective?

The novel illustrates that the combination of science and esoterism
is not a harmonious one. Beyond his literary licence and his narrative

Various ambigrams (text read from left to right, and is the same after being rotated 180 degrees). From top to bottom: Tunez, Mercedes, Mexico.

subtleties, there is in Brown's book one obvious theme: the chasm between science and the Church. The Illuminati, members of a large secret society, were born with the mission to split away from the Church, and they appear two centuries too early in the book, arriving in Brown's work as scientists:

...In the 1500s, a group of men in Rome fought back against the Church. Some of Italy's most enlightened men – physicists, mathematicians, astronomers – began meeting secretly to share their concerns about the Church's inaccurate teachings...They founded the world's first scientific think tank, calling themselves 'the enlightened ones'.

Following the story, one dark and stormy night in 1785 a solitary messenger was struck by lightning on the road from Frankfurt to Paris. The following day a Bavarian guard patrol lifted the body and found a strange document in his robes. It was entitled *Original Change in Days of Illumination*, and was signed by Esparticus, the not-so-secret pseudonym of the renegade Jesuit, Adam Weishaupt. This mysterious person, born in Ingolstadt in 1748, was the professor of Canon Law at the city's university, where, despite the opposition of the clergy, he openly discussed his messianic ideas on the necessity for a world revolution against the advancing evil.

Weishaupt was a member of the Company of Jesus and was an eminent member of the Bavarian Masons at the time. However, he had a personal vision of the world situation and considered that the Church played an adverse role in the morality and spirituality of humanity. He formed a group called the 'perfectionists' in Ingolstadt with some colleagues and students. This group proposed a radical change in the religious and cultural order, which would produce a new world governed by a universal democratic republic (the precursor of anarchy and socialism). In 1776, Weishaupt and his followers, among them Baron Adolf von Knigge, founded the secret sect of the Illuminati, which in Latin means 'enlightened', supposedly through an authentic divine right. In creating his organization the Bavarian occultist combined the two models he knew best: that of the Jesuits and that of the Masons. According to history, this lodge had a short life; it was dissolved 11 years later after the unfortunate episode with the messenger and the discovery of Weishaupt's secret document. However, different authors maintain that not only do the Illuminati exist today in an ultra-secret form, but also that they may have existed long before the accepted foundation date.

The Bavarian government banned the Illuminati in 1787, condemning to death those who tried to recruit new members for the Order or publicize Weishaupt's secret document and the conspiratorial plans of the sect.

Adam Weishaupt, creator of the Illuminati of Bavaria, whose objective was to guide human beings onto the path of simple spirituality.

Even while this edict was in force, Illuminati members were rapidly dispersing across Europe and recruiting people like the German writers Johann W. Goethe and Friedrich Nicolai, the writer and philosopher Johann Gottfried von Herder and the composer Wolfgang Amadeus Mozart. When they moved on to the United States, they received the support of George Washington and Thomas Jefferson, a fact attested to by the symbols on the reverse of the dollar bill, such as the split pyramid crowned with an all-seeing eye, which came from the hermetic symbols of the Illuminati.

Those who supported Weishaupt's sect continued their revolutionary conspiracy in secret, and made sure that the Illuminati, under the umbrella of the Masons and other lodges, infiltrated the British Parliament and the Secretariat of the Treasury of the United States, among other offices, in order to put their new world order into place – an order whose assumption of control would of necessity entail the elimination of the Vatican and its temporal powers.

IN THE LIGHT OF THE ILLUMINATI

To justify their conspiracies, deceits and eventual crimes morally, at times Illuminati members adopted the excuse that they were illuminated by God (or the Devil, depending on the plan at the time) to save humanity from evil and install a utopian new world. As well as Weishaupt's sect, there were at least two others with the same name that attained some importance, and in which Weishaupt's inspiration is evident:

• **The Enlightened**: A secret sect that has nothing to do with the Illuminati. They appeared at the turn of the 16th century, not in Rome but in the mountains of Afghanistan. The first leader was Bayezid Ansari. He was not a scientist and established a school of mystical initiation in Peshawar. His followers had to pass eight initiations to perfect themselves and attain magical powers.
• **Illuminés of Avignon**: Also not the Illuminati. They were a secret society founded in the 18th century dedicated to astrology and alchemy. They did not have a single connection with science at that time.

A WORLDLY SECT

Even though in reality the alleged followers of the Illuminati appear linked to the esoteric world, to magic and, by extension, Satanism, what becomes obvious is that all of these pursuits, as well as those linked with science, were quite remote from those of the real Illuminati.

It is certainly probable that the original Illuminati had links with secret societies with an esoteric nature (Freemasonry, the Rosicrucians and others), but their aim was very different. They were not looking for a mystical path or for the defence of scientific methods, much less to obtain magic or esoteric powers. The Illuminati's objective was, simply and clearly, to remove the existing political and religion establishments: to overthrow the governments, eliminate the concept of patriotism and, by extension, abolish religion. In order to create his secret society Weishaupt did not have to wait for a divine revelation or for the discovery of some ancestral manuscripts, or to receive the hermetic legacy of some predecessors. Unlike other orders, the Iluminati have a proven name and date in history. The Illuminati was the product of one mind, that of its founder, and from one inspiration, the kind of world in which he wanted to live.

The 18th century: A Complex Era

To understand the birth of the secret society of the Illuminati in all its magnitude, we must review the complexity of the events at the end of the 18th century.

• A century earlier, Galileo, Bacon and Descartes had created a 'new' science that threatened the Church, who then condemned it.
• It was a time of clerical supremacy over society, a Christian world that saw a serious danger in the advance of the Protestant Reformation and a very grave threat from the advances of scientific knowledge.
• In 1723 the Masons were officially founded; they continued and modernized the artistic brotherhoods of previous centuries. Those who were in dispute with the Church could find refuge in Masonry's ranks.
• The Declaration of Independence was signed in the United States. On 4 July 1776, the thirteen colonies of North America declared sovereignty and independence. The Masons and the Illuminati exerted a strong influence and participated in the event.
• In 1789 the French Revolution occurred, largely initiated by intellectuals and progressive politicians of the era. Those who participated did not agree with or belong to the long-established power, represented by the 'Old Regime' of the aristocracy and the clergy.
• Philosophical and scientific concepts changed radically: the *Encyclopaedia* of Diderot was published and the moral and conscious philosophy of Kant, the sciences of Lanmark and the creativity of artists like Goethe, Goya, Mozart, Molière and Beethoven were flourishing.

THE STRENGTH OF THE CONSPIRACY

It seems evident that Adam Weishaupt, the founder of the Illuminati, did not imagine he could actually dominate the world, at least not in the way we would think of it today. But he did envisage social dominance and broke ties with the 'usual' powers, which was the authority of the Pope and the ecclesiastical doctrines. It seems that he approached the Masons looking for people with whom he could discuss his ideas, and who could perhaps help him put them into practice. Nevertheless, the formal and anodyne ritualism of the Munich Masonic Lodge did not impress him. He had his

Portrait of Voltaire. The French writer was one of many intellectuals linked to secret societies.

own ideas about the world and what to do with it. His ambition was to create and direct his own secret society. Tired of the constant pressure that the Jesuits put on him, and disappointed by the practices of the Masons, he decided to look for something that better suited his ideas of a secret society. From this moment, the 'light' ensnared him. Knowledge was his and Truth would be his power. He tried to leave the light of the Christian religion, to spread the message of the authentic bearer of light, which was none other than 'Lucifero' – Lucifer.

Adam Weishaupt was condemned to isolation. He became more rationalist, anti-Catholic and fanatically radical, in regard to both politics and religion. He had previously been appointed curator of the University, a post the Jesuits gave him so he could reorganize the centre of studies. After his previous flirtations with the Masons, he felt he did not need them and was sure that the Illuminati should not perform rituals, because that was a defining feature of the Masons. From that moment the Illuminati made themselves into a lay institution with the goal of advancing humanity. The movement started to entice into its ranks numerous German rationalists who were attracted to the theories of French philosophers such as Voltaire and politicians like Robespierre. Both of these, in addition to their roles in history, had links with distinct secret societies: the Masons, the Rosicrucians and, in some ways, the Illuminati.

THE 'LIGHT' GOES OUT

Thus the Order of the Illuminati was a society whose intentions were far more political than mystical. Despite the fact that Adam Weishaupt seemed to have thought of everything and managed to organize his society, something had escaped him. Little by little, people who were disenchanted with Masonry were admitted by his Order and by the Rosicrucians. Perhaps they were nothing but infiltrators in these societies, rather than people looking for spiritual refuge. Leaving to one side the idea that conspiracies lay in the minds of only the conspirators, what is certain is Weishaupt's

The Final Objective of the Illuminati

The founder of the Illuminati had a clear idea about how to preserve his secret society from the beginning. In the first instance, he protected it from the outside. It was closed to the curious, and he decided that the only way for anyone to gain entry was through close contacts and trust. Only the most influential could get close to the Order. Its hierarchy was extremely rigid and the authority remained exclusively with Weishaupt himself.

The final path to the world's salvation had five essential objectives:

• The end of government: he tried to eradicate and abolish monarchies and any other form of government that did not fit with his ideas. The members of the sect, protected by its economic, social and political power, were given the task of eradicating other powers. There was only room for one government: theirs.
• The end of possessions: the goal was to ensure that the economic power resided with the members of the brotherhood and in their networks. Private property and inherited rights were a threat. The Illuminati members ensured they were in places of control where economic power was concerned.
• The end of the concept of nations: it was deemed necessary to eradiate the multiplicity of nations. One great empire, one great country, was preferable to the existance of many, which would be difficult to control. It was necessary to eliminate the concepts of patriotism and nationalism. The objective was to find a new world order. We should remember that in history Julius Caesar, like Bonaparte and Hitler, also wanted to create a single empire.
• The end of the family: the Illuminati did not believe in matrimony or in the Christian concept of the family, nor in educational systems. In part, this is logical, since those ideas came from religion. The objective was to be free of families, where love and desire of union between two people triumphed over a sacramental link to the Church. Education would be limited to communal systems where the educators were members of the Order.
• The end of religion: religious and spiritual beliefs were considered to be forms of distraction, as well as dangerous links to the power of the enemy. To eradicate religion meant that the ideas of the secret society alone would serve as hope and counsel in life.

order managed to achieve notable power – one that spread to the French Revolution, a decisive historic event in Europe, and one that, to a certain extent, could have been orchestrated by the Illuminati. Over time their power increased and could have influenced the two world wars of the 20th century and may be responsible for a third, for which, presumably, we are still waiting.

However, eight years after its foundation, although officially it was 11 years old, Weishaupt slowly let the lights that powered his sect go out. This was not a voluntary act but an enforced one. The Bavarian government, observing the strength of the Illuminati and their open public activity, which had not only grown but also extended to members across the Atlantic, decided that they were a dangerous threat. Weishaupt lost his professorship and, immediately afterwards, was expelled from the country. Officially the Order ended, although in reality it merely disbanded. Its founder went to live in exile, taking refuge in one of the many properties of one of his protectors, Duke Ernst von Gotha, where he stayed until his death on 18 November 1830.

However, history does not end with the disbanding of the Illuminati. After the Order was dissolved, its founder continued for several decades to form conspiracies and demonstrate to his brothers and followers the noble art of secret societies. Weishaupt wrote various works, among them a chronicle on the persecution of the Illuminati in Bavaria, a manual on Illuminism, as well as various tracts on the advantages of his doctrinal principles. He also found time to keep up links with leaders of the Masons, and other secret orders, at the start of the 19th century.

THE OCCULT MARK OF THE ILLUMINATI

'Sometimes, it is necessary for darkness to reign for a moment before a new splendour', Weishaupt said in one of his texts. The Illuminati lit just one of the many torches that made up the blaze of secret societies. They reappeared at an opportune moment, and although they were not the original members, the many plots and conspiracies of the original sect were doubtless a strong influence on this group later in history.

Occasionally the error is made of believing that the end or suspension of a secret entity brings definitive death. This error has been made by many in respect to the Illuminati. Officially they lasted eleven years. The historic version confirms that the society was disbanded, and that its founder fled and died in exile. Nevertheless, for conspiracy theorists that was not the end, but rather the beginning of a new era. Despite the fact that the group was officially dead, they managed to continue with their activities in a more clandestine way and did not have to worry about pretending they did not exist.

There is another aspect to bear in mind, which is that the Illuminati managed to gain positions of power in other apparently more innocent secret societies, like for example the Rosicrucians and the Masons.

As the Illuminati broke up, the ranks of the Masons grew, as did those of the Rosicrucians and other smaller secret sects, like the Carbonari or the society that in Spain is known as the Santa Garduña. Other theories state the reverse, that it was the Masons who, on merging with the Illuminati, oversaw its final destruction.

It is evident that only one of the two theories can be correct, and it is interesting to note that a society like the Masons, in principle a spiritual order, made a series of political moves that were suspiciously Illuminist. One of these theories – the more likely one – indicated that, in reality, after the apparent dissolution of the Illuminati it reformed and grew as a secret society within another. Within Masonry there was another brotherhood, so secret that even other Masons were unaware of it, made up of Masonic brothers who also belonged to the Illuminati. According to this theory they dominated both societies, and aimed to dominate the world.

At this point, it is worth asking: what other secret societies influenced and participated in the Illuminati's conspiracy? What link do Masonry, the Carbonari and the Santa Garduña have to the events that caused the upheavals of the Enlightenment and the 19th century? Were the Illuminati really gone, or were they watching closely and participating actively in the independence of the British Colonies and in the French Revolution?

While not trying to demean the validity of the plot of *Angels and Demons*, it is in fact an innocent child's game compared with what has gone on in the past, and also very possibly with the reality of the present day.

4. Other Powerful Secret Societies and Groups

If you seek new results, do not always do the same thing.
Albert Einstein

It is essential for any secret society to remain invisible to the eyes of the world. Therefore, public prudence and discretion were basic components of their existence. Nevertheless, in centuries past and present, old and new brotherhoods and powerful secret groups have started to act almost in the light of day. It is a bit surprising that they are still called secret, when they are openly talk about and publicly debated, their intentions are discussed and their activities form bestselling plots. The Illuminati, the Rosicrucians and the Masons are perhaps some of the most popular in the real secret societies 'hit parade'.

The choice is simple: either shadow governments, the ones who really make all the important decisions, exist within those societies, trying to remain secret, or the secret societies are in fact no more than a cover for other groups that have not yet been uncovered.

Aside from the conspiratorial 'classic' societies that we have mentioned, many others have existed and still exist which, in their own way, did not want to participate in world domination or in great universal decisions, but to concentrate on more specific goals. Some have specialized in dominating economies, others in religion, others in determining social movements and many of them have attained influence in those countries where they were established.

THE APOSTLES OF THE DEVIL

The Luciferians were a group founded by Gualterio Lollard in the 14th century. They claimed that Lucifer and his angels represented knowledge and wisdom. They maintained that the image imposed upon them by the Church was unjust and, by extension, so was the expulsion of Lucifer and his angels from Heaven, as well as how they were presented in the sacred texts. This society,'s member, who endeavoured to be seekers of knowledge and became completely opposed to the decrees of Rome, spread throughout the Netherlands, Germany, Austria, France and England.

We must not confuse the Luciferians with the followers of a group called the 'Doorway of the Light with Satan', which is an evil entity. There are two diabolical currents against the established Church: the theoretical, intellectual and reflective one of Luciferism; and the practical, mundane, earthly, dictatorial and hierarchal movement of Satanism.

Satanism sought to attack the Church, invert its symbols and profane its temples. It tried, simply and plainly, to maintain a line of action totally opposed to what came from Rome. It is described as a 'fight against the opposition'. Nevertheless, Satanism would not make sense if the Church did not exist; it would not have a single enemy, at least from the conceptual point of view, if it could not turn to Evil or more specifically to Satan, the counter-figure to God. Neither Church no Satanism, that is, the

Antique sketch of the Fallen Angel. According to Luciferians he represents knowledge and wisdom.

representations of Good and Bad, would not have enough reason to be if the other did not exist.

Luciferians sought clarity and intellect. It was based on the idea that Lucifer faced up to God by refusing to give up wisdom, free judgement and free will. They asserted that human beings are very much like the representation of Lucifer, since they have senses, emotions, sensibilities, souls and dreams. Like him, they try to understand how the world began and who God is, and to require a liberty that is not subjugated to designs of entities that they do not understand.

It is unsurprising that, in the light of theories like these, Dan Brown had the idea that the Illuminati, in a certain way, have a Luciferian link, given their quest for knowledge, in this case defending the supremacy of science over dogma. We must make clear that Luciferism does not resort, like Satanism does, to violence and the breaking of governmental and civil laws.

THE OTHER CONSPIRACIES

In the wake of the French Revolution and the Napoleonic invasions, 19th-century Europe became a fertile breeding ground for secret societies and conspiratorial groups, some of which were played important roles in the significant political and social changes of the century. It would be difficult to mention all of them, but here is a brief account of the most important:

• **The Carbonari**. The secret society of the Carbonari emerged in the south of Italy during the Napoleonic occupation. Its symbol was coal, which they saw as 'capable of purifying the air and distancing them from the dwellings of ferocious beasts'. They thought that, like the combustible element it was, coal had the ability to clean the surrounding atmosphere and, therefore, allow human beings to approach the problems that preoccupy them from fresh points of view. They thought coal, used in ritual ceremonies, would favour mental clarity and eliminate their enemies, who were politicians, religious leaders and the military, those whom they called 'ferocious beasts'.

The Carbonari movement emerged in Naples at the start of the 19th century and also operated in France, Portugal and Spain. Their basic ideology was to fight against civil and religious authorities. Their mission was based on reaching a level of freedom where they could give their opinion on the established powers. They met in secret in small shacks that, when grouped together, began to be called 'republics'. The members, from the upper and upper-middle classes, were organized in a hierarchy of lodges that maintained a parallel structure, which was bounded, on one side, by the civil population and on the other, by the armed forces.

Although it was a secret society that possessed esoteric roots, some of its members had relations with Masonry and the Illuminati, because the Carbonari group was a conspiratorial society of political character. Amongst its more renowned members was Giuseppe Garibaldi, the great fighter for the independence and union of Italy; and Giuseppe Mazzini, the former's mentor and founder of the revolutionary lodge of 'Young Italy', which was linked to other secretive libertarian societies. Their conspiracies were carried on in a series of letters that Mazzini exchanged with Albert Pike, the founder of the Ku Klux Klan.

Reproduction of the Statute of the Carbonari (photo from the Museum of the Italian Renaissance.)

• **La Santa Garduña**. Their legendary origin is dated to before the emergence of the Illuminati (in the 18th century). It started as a guerrilla and political group, while also in some ways, a mystical one. According to the legend of its foundation, after the Arab invasion of Spain, St Apolinario, a devoted hermit, experienced a vision of the Virgin of Cordoba. The apparition warned him that the Muslim invasion was a divine punishment for carelessness and neglgencee with regard to religious observance. The Virgin warned St Apolinario to bring together good people in his name, and teach them to live by the Bible and take up the mission of attacking the Arabic invaders, their possessions and their families.

Giuseppe Garibaldi, one of the more active and renowned members of the Carbonari.

Although the official history situates the secret movement of La Garduña in the 19th century, chronicles mention that their predecessors were already active in the 16th and 17th centuries as secret collaborators in the Inquisition, participating in the executions of Arabs and Jews and acquisition of their goods. The Garduñas used the Bible as an oracle. Before planning an attack or making a decision, they opened the sacred book of fate and looked for an inspirational phrase or passage, and then went into action.

In more modern times, the Garduñas emerged as a political group who supported the resistance against Napoleonic domination. After the French retreat, they became a liberal society comprised of affluent and influential members. Their power and interference was notable, so much so that in 1821 the government of the Spanish King Fernando VII detained the Grand Master Francisco de Cortina, in an attempt to suppress the Order.

On 25th November 1822, Cortina and 16 other agents of the Order were executed in Seville. This act prompted the survivors to go underground, and many fled to South America where they re-established the Order and took part in struggles for independence.

Masonry had an influence on the emancipation of a good part of the Spanish colonies. The Freemason Francisco de Miranda tried to start disturbances in Venezuela; Simon Bolívar and José de San Martín were

Masons, and in 1810 the Hidalgo and Castillo Masons started the
independence movement in Mexico, and members of the Santa Garduña
were supposedly in close collaboration with them, realizing that many of
these actions gave them opportunities to achieve their own goals.

A Mercenary Order

The Santa Garduña was organized into nine grades, led by the
members of the 'Master' grade.

Each Master coordinated the members of a group of mercenaries who,
in this case, were instructed to assassinate, rob, kidnap and extort
money or goods from Arabic and Jewish citizens and followers of the
other religions.

They were compensated with set rewards. In that way, by contracting
their services, they could charge different amounts for whether they
needed to pressurize, extort from, kidnap or kill.

Once paid for the services, in kind or in coin, a third of the amount was
shared between the mercenaries and the rest passed to the
organization, ensuring that the money or possessions served to
perpetuate and extend their power

• **The Powerful Black Knights**. This is a clandestine society influenced
by the Illuminati and with certain links to the Masons. It was a local order
founded in 1815 by a professor from Berlin, with the object of fighting
against the invasion of the Napoleonic power. It is questionable whether
the Masons were involved in this group, given that Napoleon himself was
part of the Masonic lodge of Hermes.

• **The Commoners**. The Commoners were a secret society that started in
1821 in the heart of Masonry, and took the name of the Castillian
Commoners who had resisted Emperor Charles I in the 16th century. The
new Commoners affirmed that their essential object was to conserve, with
all the power in their reach, the liberty of the human race, and the rights of
the Spanish masses against abuse of power, as well as helping those who
had been disgraced because of the cause.

• **The Concienciarios**: Enemies of the Church. Although in theory an
association of progressive thinkers, everything seems to indicate that on the

inside was a secret group of notable free-thinkers, with something of a Satanist view as they denied the existence of God. On the surface they were a Protestant group with local influence, who in 1764 in Paris proclaimed some of their explicit beliefs: God does not exist, neither does the Devil.

The Concienciarios scorned members of the Church, who they considered manipulators. They insisted that science and reason had to replace priests and magistrates. Their philosophy of action was:

• To live honestly united to a global awareness of all, rejecting everything governed by the sacred texts, especially the Bible which, in their opinion, was full of 'fables and contradictions'.
• Not to hurt anything or anyone, except when necessary.
• To influence the governing classes in order to refine society, to demonstrate that those concepts imposed upon man by the Church, like family and matrimony, were nothing but limitations for happiness and the elevation of the human being.

• **The Decembrists**: aristocratic conspirators. Again, this is a presumably secret local group, although supposedly influenced by Illuminati ideas, and formed by Russian nobles, who questioned the tsar's absolutism and were in favour of a constitutional monarchy. Because of the group's economic power, they managed to rise to positions of influence in Russian politics. The name came from the date of their first revolt, the 21 December 1825, an attempt to prevent Tsar Nicholas II from gaining the throne. The riot was cruelly repressed and the Decembrists became even more secretive. Nevertheless their underground activity continued to be intense. They founded various secret groups as offshoots of the Order – 'the Society of the North', 'the Society of the United Slaves' and 'the Society of the South' for example. It is believed that they later disbanded into smaller secret groups.

Portrait of Nicholas II. The revolution of the Decembrists did not impede his ascent to the throne; most of them were finally exiled to Siberia or executed.

• **The White Sons of Ireland**. A local group of Irish conspirators, whose first testimonials date from 1761. A secret society inspired by the Freemasonry, as much for their organizational structure as for their determination to reach political levels of power. They had two branches: one more contemplative and speculative that flirted with esoterism and initiated spirituality; the other much tougher, anxious to engage in action against the established power, known for burning houses and attacking larg properties. They challenged the imposed religious norms, defending the liberty of man from inside the mandates of divinity.

5. Secret Plots for Real Worlds

The study of politics is employed in covering the face of the lie, which
appears to be the truth, hiding the deceit and disguising the designs.
Diego de Saavedra

Politics is the art of serving men making believe that it serves them.
Louis Dumbur

Secret societies have been accused of supporting events like the American
War of Independence, the French Revolution, the uprisings that
precipitated the independence of the South American countries, the Soviet
Revolution, the world wars, the fall of the Berlin wall and Gorbachev's
Perestroika, not to mention the more recent conflicts like the crisis in the
Persian Gulf that provoked the two wars in Iraq. Before confirming that all
these events stemmed from secret societies' plots and interests, we should
leave a space for all the doubts and good faith. But what is true is that the
facts with which we tell this story are rather difficult to believe.

1789: THE YEAR OF CHANGE

The French Revolution did not happen overnight. It grew slowly by means
of schemes and plots that culminated, at least broadly speaking, in the
overthrow of Louis XVI, the end of the monarchy in France and the
proclamation of the First Republic.

It is significant that the slogan of the Freemasons of the Lodge of
France was 'Liberty, equality, fraternity' long before the Revolution,
because, of course, this was adopted as the ideological motto of the
Revolution's instigators. Everything seems to indicate that the intellectuals,
financiers and politicians who were members of secret societies, were very
interested in putting into place a plot capable of changing the dominant
social and political structures.

The Scottish rite of Masonry was introduced into France in the
middle of the 18th century by soldiers and aristocrats. There were

Illuminati among their ranks and they were perfectly infiltrated into society. Despite Louis XVI's threatening incarceration in the Bastille for anyone who belonged to secret societies, (which were becoming increasingly dangerous), their numbers continued to grow.

Masonic ideology was very attractive to a downtrodden and impoverished population. It is estimated that in the days before the Revolution there were around 60,000 Masons in France. This is a significant number, if we keep in mind that they occupied the highest levels of the bourgeoisie and were virtually at the top of the circles where new ideas and opinions were made. If we add to this that the mission of the Illuminati was the eradication of monarchy, the abolition of private property and the elimination of the power of the clergy, one can argue convincingly that the Illuminati were a significant influence in the Revolution.

Another important fact is the large number of strategic changes occurring within many Masonic Lodges; they radicalized their political stance and planned to bring down the monarchy and the government. At this time societies like 'The Friends of Truth' were being formed, destined to come up with a social reform plan that inspired the French Revolution. Another society, called 'Of the Nine Sisters', sought the creation of an

alternative education system to to the then-current clerical model. People who initiated the fight for American independence actively participated in such organizations. Leaders like Benjamin Franklin , philosophers led by Voltaire and esoterics like the Count of Cagliostro or Dr Franz Mesmer, author of the theory of animal magnetism, were all members of such groups.

After the revolutionary uprising of 1789, the National Assembly was set up – with 80 per cent of the members being Masons. The aims of the Revolution were religious liberty, the annulment of the rights of the monarchy and the declaration of the rights of man. They aimed to set up a

Giuseppe Bálsamo (known as Cagliostro), Rosicrucian, mystic and healer and creator of the Masonic rite of the three grades.

popular militia, with an élite guard infiltrated and controlled by members of the principle secret societies had infiltrated, with the mission of keeping watch over security and clandestinely working in aid of the fundamental belief of their groups.

Some secret societies that supported the French Revolution from the outset were not entirely satisfied with the final outcome. Although the first change intended was the establishment of a constitutional monarchy, the mob appeared to be taking over, which was not the intention of the

---

The Mysterious Count of Cagliostro

The person known as Cagliostro, born in Palermo in 1743, was in reality called Giuseppe Bálsamo. He was born into a humble family and was more or less raised in the street, which taught him how to survive on his wits in order to triumph over adversity. He travelled to the main cultural centres of that time: Greece, Egypt, Morocco, Spain and France, as well as within Italy. These were all centres of study for the mystical and the occult. In those times Cagliostro lived by swindling and travelled widely throughout Europe selling an 'elixir of eternal youth', a product he combined with love philtres and useless alchemic potions.

By 1785 he was living and idle existence in the French court, but after a scandal linking him to the theft of Marie Antoinette's necklace, he began to fall from grace. In 1791 he was detained by the Inquisition, accused of deceit, fraud and, most importantly of all, of being a conspirator and member of the Masons, as well as trying to organize a Lodge in Italy. It is perfectly true that Cagliostro had connections with the Rosicrucians and had introduced major reforms to the rites of this secret society. He was also a member of the Masons and among his most influential prophecies were those predicting the French Revolution and the Independence of the United States. The Masonic lodge which had welcomed the mysterious count, was later involved in both events.

The official line is that Cagliostro remained in prison until his death. However, according to legend, not only did he make temporary trips out of the prison by means of a magic mirror, he also used his wizard powers to flee prison. Another version says that he magically swapped his body with that of a monk (or a guard), and that the body the guards found and proclaimed to be Cagliostro actually belonged to the monk or guard.

Many Freemasons died at the hands of the wretched invention of one of their 'brothers', Dr Guillotin

'shadow' government'. The first Republic was proclaimed and Louis XVI and his family were imprisoned. In 1793 the king was sentenced to death and beheaded, as were hundreds of others. They were beheaded using the invention of doctor (and mason) Joseph Ignace Guillotin's invention, commonly known as 'Mme Guillotine'.

Confronted with this unexpected and alarming situation, the shadow government had to find someone amongst their acolytes who could take control. Who better than the bright General Napoleon, popular hero and faithful Mason?

NAPOLEON BONAPARTE, A LUCKY MASON

In the year that the king was beheaded, Corsica declared its independence from France. Bonaparte, who was a lieutenant colonel in the French National Guard, fled to the continent with his family. That moment would be a milestone in his meteoric career. He was promoted to the rank of general at twenty-four and two years later saved the revolutionary government from a revolt in Paris. In 1796 he fought against Austria and her allies, and in the name of France he conquered and named the Cisalpine, Ligurian and Transalpine Republics. Shortly after, he led an expedition to Egypt, which was then under Turkish rule. He conquered it and reformed the Egyptian administration and legal system. He abolished slavery and feudalism and left in place a group of French experts to study the ancient history of Egypt and carry out archaeological excavations.

On returning to France, Napoleon joined a conspiracy against the Jacobin government and took part in the November 1799 coup d'état. A new regime was established in which Napoleon virtually had absolute power. In 1802 a constitution was created and two years later, when nearly all of Europe had fallen to him, he proclaimed himself emperor.

To conspiracy theorists, Napoleon's Europe and the empire that he managed to build was made possible only thanks to the wise intervention of several members of the Illuminati. Although Napoleon Bonaparte's purpose was simply to form a European federation of free nations, one must not forget that this ancient society's aim was always to establish a global government.

THE RETURN OF THE MEROVINGIAN KINGS

It was not only the Masons and the Illuminati who had an interest in Napoleon. A less known and even stranger secret society was scheming behind the Emperor's back to return the French throne to the first kings of France, the Merovingian dynasty, and to dominate the whole of Europe.

The names of the main group behind the plot will sound familiar to readers of Dan Brown's first book, *The Da Vinci Code*: the Priory of Syon, the secret brotherhood and precursor of the Order of the Poor Knights of Christ, better known as The Order of the Temple.

It appears that the Templars had a mission to preserve the lineage of royal blood carried by the daughter of Jesus and Mary Magdalene, and whose descendants formed the Merovingian dynasty of kings. The idea is not only anachronistic but is also somehow implausible.

Meroveo, the legendary barbarian leader, whose name was used by the dynasty established in Gaul, was a pagan of Germanic origin who could have had little or nothing to do with the supposed descendents of Jesus. But in history, we always have to bear in mind that anything is possible.

NAPOLEON AND HIS MEROVINGIAN WIFE

Napoleon was unaware of his proximity to the Merovingian bloodline. It is believed that members of the Priory of Syon arranged an 'accidental' meeting between Napoleon and Josephine. The arrangement was kept alive with the help of clairvoyants and sorcerers who together conspired to make it happen with marriage as an end result.

Marie-Josèphe Rose Tascher de la Pagerie, commonly known as Josephine, was the widow of Viscount Beauharnais, who had been beheaded during the Revolution. They had two children, Eugene and Hortense, who belonged to the Merovingian dynasty, an inheritance from their father's family. Through this marriage and the later adoption of the children by Napoleon, the Merovingian dynasty returned to the French throne. The union was further cemented when Hortense married Louis I Bonaparte, Napoleon's brother, and gave birth to the second French emperor, Napoleon III.

CHRISTOPHER COLUMBUS DID NOT COME FIRST

By now, no matter how much traditionalists argue, it is naïve to maintain that Christopher Columbus discovered America. The inhabitants of those lands had long been expecting the return of the Viracochas, the white gods who had once visited in the past.

Josephine, anonymous portrait. According to legend, her marriage with Bonaparte was orchestrated by the Priory of Syon to perpetuate the Merovingian dynasty

One story says that the first Europeans arrived in the New World as early as 877. It was a group of Irish monks belonging to the Culdeans, a secret order with no historical record. The Vikings followed, arriving in Canada first, then travelling as far south Mexico and other parts of Central America. It is believed by some that the Vikings drew later the maps of the New World used by Columbus on his travels. Some chronicles say these maps would end up in the hands of the military order of the Temple who,

Jesus' Descendants

According to the records in 1099 Godfrey of Bouillon established the Order of Syon after conquering Jerusalem. Its mission was the preservation of the pure blood of descendants of Mary Magdalene and Jesus. This Christological belief says that Mary Magdalene left for the Gaul with Joseph of Arimathea. She took the Holy Grail with her but not in the form of a communion cup – Mary Magdalene was pregnant and carried Jesus' blood inside her.

Once in France Jesus' descendents arranged a marriage with the family of the first king of the Franks. This is how the Merovingian dynasty was created. The Priory of Syon continued with its secret mission, taking care of the blood royal until an appropriate time came for a Merovingian descendant to recuperate the throne of France.

feeling threatened after the fall of the Kingdom of Jerusalem in 1187, decided to negotiate with the Vikings to ensure they were established in the New World. Together they planned the first route to take them there, a long time before Columbus' voyage. It was also before Columbus that the members of the Priory of Syon, who were in charge of protecting the blood royal, took refuge in America.

There is also another very curious detail worth taking into account: in 1446 the Count of Saint Clair, who had an excellent relationship with the Knights Templar, gave instructions to build a chapel 10 kilometres (6 miles) from Edinburgh. As well as a variety of esoteric symbols sculpted on the walls of the chapel an ear of corn and other American plants were then unknown in Europe also appear. The official date for the discovery of America is 12 October 1492, 42 years after the chapel was consecrated.

REFUGE IN AMERICA

After the discovery of America, the first settlers to arrive had more than one motive to enrol in this transatlantic adventure. The strongest reason would probably have been the persecution they suffered in Europe.

There were many people in Spain, France, Portugal, England, Italy and other European kingdoms persecuted, by the establishment. They saw in the New World an escape and the possibility of a new life and a fresh start. These people had a common background, condemnation in their homelands for their religious, political or philosophical beliefs and for committing common crimes. Countless were pardoned but in return had to

Portrait of Benjamin Franklin, an American leader who was also a Freemason

settle in the colonies. Many among them prepared the grounds for the clandestine continuation of secret societies and their conspiracies. One of the secret societies was the Order of the Quest supposedly established in America in 1625; Benjamin Franklin was later amongst its members. The Order of the Helmet linked to the Knights Templar, was another one. The Masons, the Illuminati and the Rosicrucians arrived later.

CONSPIRACY AND THE FOUNDATION OF THE UNITED STATES

The Illuminati's ultimate objective had always been to create a new world order. The New World looked like the perfect place to achieve this. All leads seem to point to the fact that the Illuminati managed to build a network with their own resources or using other secret societies in order to achieve what has been known as the 'secret destiny of the United States'. The Order of the Helmet played a very important role here too. A fascinating character mentioned earlier was among their members: the English philosopher Francis Bacon who was linked to sorcery, esotericism, Hermetic philosophy and the Rosicrucian movement. Many occultists believe Bacon was one of many earlier incarnations of the Count of Saint-Germain, who was supposed to be immortal.

Portrait of the Count of Saint-Germain, a mysterious and enigmatic character whose legend has stayed alive.

The legend begins in the surroundings of the Carpathian Mountains where Saint-Germain was born on 26 May 1696. Apparently he may have been the son of the last Transylvanian king. Some say he was the original Count Dracula. Saint-Germain studied and excelled in Kabbala and alchemy and acquired magical powers. In 1758 Madame de Pompadour grew interested in his feats and decided she wanted to meet him. After their first encounter she felt 'captivated by his strength and power, capable of showing incredible wonders to simple mortals'. She then introduced him to Louis XV and his entourage.

What most fascinated the courtiers was that, apart from looking 30 at 62, he never ate or drank and no one ever saw him sleep or even grow tired. He was also always splendidly dressed and he was wealthy but no one knew where this wealth came from. Rumours spread that he possessed incredible alchemic secrets that gave him the power to transform lead into gold. But this is just one small detail of his long, mysterious life.

At this period, just before the Declaration of Independence and subsequent creation of the United States of America, the Catholic Church and various secret societies, particularly the Illuminati, were involved in a power struggle. The clergy was doing as much as possible to spread Catholicism in the New World and the secret societies saw this as a menace to their own plans. During this period, Freemasons settled comfortably in the 13 British provinces of the continent, so favouring the later development of a great number of new orders that had their own political, social and economic interests.

The beginning of 1776 saw the colonies gradually overpower their British sovereign who, unable to cope with the struggle, ended up abandoning them. The Declaration of Independence of the 13 British

THE COUNT OF SAINT-GERMAIN: IMMORTAL CONSPIRATOR

These are some of the great deeds attributed to Saint-Germain through his never-ending life:
• He inspired Akhenaten by starting a new monotheistic cult.
• He was one of the Temple of Solomon's builders and, given his immortality, centuries later he worked with the cathedral builders encouraging them to create an original society that would later become the Freemasonry.
• He was one of the main instigators of the Rosicrucian movement. Some even say that he was Christian Rosenkreutz himself.
• It has even been alleged that he was the English philosopher and scientist Roger Bacon (1214–1294) and that he participated and collaborated in investigations carried out by geniuses like Leonardo da Vinci (1452–1519) or Galileo Galilei.
• He handed over some secret maps to Columbus, which consequently guided the latter to the Americas making possible their consequent discovery.
• He inspired Adam Weishaupt to create the Illuminati of Baviera and followed their movements very closely when they joined the Freemasonry.

Saint-Germain actively participated in the independence of the English colonies in America through different secret societies and helped create the United States of America.

colonies of North America was made effective on 4 July. All together, 53 out of the 56 who signed the declaration were Masons.

IN THE NAME OF THE DOLLAR

After Independence, there was a need to create new symbols for a new nation. One of the most prominent was the dollar. Analysis of some aspects of this currency and its symbols is intriguing.

The initial monetary law that the Federal Government established was to have two value standards: a silver dollar and a gold dollar, which would only be in circulation between 1849 and 1889. They also started using the decimal system at that time because they found it easier than the British system. But the most curious thing is that the dollar bill's design, still in use today, was made following assement and advice from both the Masons' and the Illuminati's:

Many of the symbols that appear on dollar bills have a Masonic or
Illuminati origin

• The phoenix was the winged creature on the first dollars. It symbolized
resurrection from the ashes, leaving the past behind and letting the future
flourish, but it was also a Hermetic symbol.
• In 1841 the eagle, an Egyptian symbol of the sun, replaced the Phoenix,
until then the avian national symbol of the United States. The tale says that
originally the phoenix's tail was red and blue, the colours of the United
States' flag
• The 13 stars represent the 13 states of that time. The five-pointed stars
are a Masonic symbol.
• The eagle on the dollar has 9 feathers in its taleil and this matches the
number of grades of the Masonic ritual of York prevalent at the time in
America. Its wings have 32 and 33 feathers each, corresponding to the
grades in the Scottish rite.
• To symbolize spirituality, reflection and thought, the eagle holds an olive
branch with his right foot. With the left he holds 13 arrows representing
action and transmutation.

• The depiction of both feet is an allegory symbolizing the struggle between conflicting yet interdependant forces. Therefore, they represent light and dark; war and peace; openness and obstinacy; both the sense of being public and private.

• The eagle carries in its beak a parchment with the Latin inscription *E Pluribus Unum*. This is a clear allusion to the call for the integration and unity of those belonging to the old colonies that now formed one nation. It could also be read as a call for the unification of all nations into one, in accordance with Illuminati doctrine.

• On the left side of the dollar is the favourite symbol of the Illuminati. It is a truncated pyramid with the apex raised. It has 1776, in Roman numerals, on its base. This is the year of the Declaration of Independence. On the top of the pyramid there is a triangle with an eye in the middle. This is an Illuminati symbol that would later appear on the Masons' coat of arms.

• The eye shining in the triangle is a metaphor of the Illuminati being in all places at all times, with a clear view and no chance of error; like God.

• On the top of the eye it says *Annuit Coeptis*, which can be translated as 'he favours our establishment'. This is clearly an indication that the Illuminati objectives have been achieved: they are at the top.

• The words *Novus Ordo Seculorum* encircle the pyramid. This translates as 'new secular order', while conspiracy theorists translate it as 'new world order'.

• In the middle of the note, just above the word 'One', it says 'IN GOD WE TRUST'. This seems contradictory to the non-religious character of the orders of that period but could also be interpreted more controversially as a statement that divinity does not just belong to one specific religion.

• The detail of the pyramid has been intentionally left until last. Firstly we can see that it is made of 72 stones. Some interpret this as the 72 steps in Jacob's ladder linked to Judaism and Kabbala. On the other hand, the pyramid is unfinished which may imply that the country is under construction and there are no limits for achievement. A further detail is that, because it has been truncated, it is missing the great capstone supposed to project energy and attract cosmic powers.

The power of the conspirators and the secret societies arrived in the American continent. The land of the New World Order was born with the creation of the dollar.

THE FUTURE, AS DESIGNED IN THE 19TH CENTURY

Could we be experiencing the beginnings of the Third World War? To answer this we must go back in time to realize that the worst is still to come. We need to revert to the end of the 19th century. The third great war to involve all cultures in this world has already been foretold by two Illuminati members in a letter sent on 15 August 1871. This letter is kept at the British Museum in London and it is one of many letters of correspondence between two high-profile Illuminati members. It defines procedures required to carry out three world wars that will result in a new era, a new order, and a new world.

Albert Pike and Giuseppe Mazzini were high-profile Illuminati members. They frequently corresponded, making conspiracies. Pike, the author of this particular letter, as well as being an Illuminati member, was a Mason. Mazzini, also an Illuminati member, was linked to the revolutionary Risorgimento Italiano and the secret society, the Carbonari.

Albert Pike (1809–1891) was a Confederate general during the American Civil War. As a Mason he held the rank of Supreme Great General Inspector in the United States from 1859 until his death. His links to secret societies and the esoteric do not stop here, he also wrote *Morals and Dogmas of the Masonry*. Furthermore, it is believed that he was linked to another society called The Commoners. Mazzini was also a member of this society.

Albert Pike, an leading member of the Illuminati and the Freemasons. He was also the founder of the Ku Klux Klan

Mazzini (1805–1872) was a politician who, on finishing his law studies, dedicated himself to realizing the union of Italy and to eliminating any traces of foreign rule from the country. He led republican political movements against the absolutism of the Restoration monarchy. In 1828, Mazzini joined the Carbonari and ended up in prison for helping them to carry out the failed insurrection of 1821. In 1831 he founded 'La Joven Italia', (Young Italy), a revolutionary political movement repressed by the police in Piedmont the following year. Mazzini, only 27, was sentenced to death and became a

Giuseppe Mazzini, Giuseppe Garibaldi's mentor and founder of the revolutionary lodge of Young Italy fugitive fleeing first to Marseilles and later to London. Together with other young nationalist exiles he founded a secret society called 'Young Europe' in 1834 with the aim of unifying the whole of Europe in a republican confederation.

DEATH KNOCKS THREE TIMES

What is peculiar about Albert Pike's letter is that it contains indications of how things should be developed to successfully reach the Illuminati's goals: to begin three world wars and give rise to a new world order that will result in a world based on plurality and democracy. The Illuminati planned the outbreak of these three terrible conflicts as follows:

1. PREPARING THE FIRST WORLD WAR

The actual conflict started on 28 July 1914. At first it looked like a confrontation between the Austro-Hungarian Empire and Serbia but it resulted in the involvement of 32 nations. It is important to emphasize that Great Britain, France, Italy, the United States and Russia, known as the 'Allied Powers', fought against the so-called 'Central Powers', Germany, Austria-Hungary, the Ottoman Empire and Bulgaria. The war ended in 1918. Apart from the large numbers of fatalities, this war resulted in a territorial restructuring.

The following section of the letter, written in 1871 – 43 years before this world war started, indicates what the Illuminati hoped to achieve with this conflict:

...The First World War should enable the Illuminati to seize power from the tsars and transform this country with the strength of communist atheism.

The differences between the British and German empires, and also the struggle between the Germanic and Slavic nations, instigated by the Illuminati, should be used to incite this war.

Once finished, communism should be nurtured and used to destroy other governments and make religions weak...

The text was quite a prophecy. On 17 March 1917, the Russian Revolution forced Tsar Nicholas II to abdicate. Communism was born. In addition, the purpose of the war was also to break the ideological bouds between the Germanic nations. The end of the First World War meant that Germany would have to surrender part of its territory to Belgium, Czechoslovakia, Denmark, France and Poland. The Slavic nations were also profoundly affected by the changes.

Photograph of a trench during the First World War. The conflict killed more than eight million and left six million disabled

The Slavs are the largest ethnic group in Europe. Today they occupy the Balkans, the Ural Mountains, Belarus, Russia, the Ukraine, Poland, the Czech Republic, Slovakia, Serbia, Croatia and Bulgaria. A look at the territorial redistribution of Europe after the First World War shows that the disintegration of the Slavic powers was an complete success.

2. THE SECOND WORLD WAR

If the description of the first conflict's plans seems extraordinary, the plans for the Second World War, which started in 1939, will have the same effect. What began as a conflict between Germany and the coalition of Great Britain and France ended with half the world involved.

Furthermore what began as a European war ended up involving the United States, the then Soviet Union and later Asia and Africa. The conflict was not over until 1945. From then on there was a 'new world order' dominated by the Soviet Union on one side and the United States on the other. Both powers had the support of their respective satellite countries and allies and a very long 'cold war' would begin.

Referring back to Pike's 'prophetic' letters, 68 years before, he described the necessity of war and its objectives.

*...The Second World War should be incited by political discrepancies
between fascists and Zionists.
The fight should begin to destroy Nazism and give way to political Zionism
to facilitate the establishment of the sovereign state of Israel in Palestine.
During the Second World War a Communist League strong enough to equal
the whole of Christianity should be constructed. From then on it should be
kept and supported until needed the day the social cataclysm arrives...*

The Second World War meant the end of Nazism and, of course, the birth
of the State of Israel, which was declared on the 14th May 1948.

At the end of the 19th century the number of Jews in Palestine
was testament in itself: there are accounts of 12,000 in 1845, whereas in
1914 the numbers had increased to 85,000. After the First World War the
League of Nations, gave the Palestinian Mandate to the British to rule and
prepare the future State of Israel.

The British dominated the region until 1948, by when the Jewish
population had increased ten-fold, especially after 1930 following the
persecution suffered at the hands of Nazi Germany. In 1947, after the war,
the situation had worsened for the British and they had to renounce a

Photograph of the 'Big Three' at the Conference in Yalta (from left to right: Winston S.
Churchill, Franklin D. Roosevelt and Josef Stalin)

number of their powers in the Palestinian territories. The British decided to take advice from the international community and on 29 November 1947 the United Nations decided to draw up a plan to divide Palestine into an Arab and a Jewish state and make Jerusalem an international zone ruled by the UN.

Another of Pike's objectives was to build a powerful communist bloc. The First World War saw the end of the tsars followed by the Second World War and the expansion of the old Soviet Union.

Stalin, along with Roosevelt and Churchill, respective leaders of the United States and the United Kingdom, met in Tehran in 1943 to put together the military and political strategy to draw up Europe's post-war future. Later on there were to be other meetings like those at Yalta and Postdam. As a consequence of these discussions a number of zones of occupation were established in Europe. The eastern area was given over to the Soviet Union and this is how the then East Germany ended up under the influence of the Soviet Communism. Other countries such as Yugoslavia, Czechoslovakia, Romania, Bulgaria, part of Poland and areas of East Prussia suffered the same fate. The Illuminati's plan to build a strong Communist League had become a reality.

3. TOWARDS A THIRD WORLD WAR

The last piece of the Illuminati puzzle remains in the future. There is no clear date on which one could say a new world conflict started, but on 11 September 1990 George Bush, Snr talked of the need to create a new world order. This statement was made just before the first Gulf War.

Another possible date would be 11 September 2001 and the terrorist attack on the Twin Towers in New York, and Washington. In fact many newspaper headlines used the concept of a third world war to explain what had happened. We cannot be sure if the invasion of Afghanistan, the attack on the Twin Towers and the Israel-Palestine conflict are part of a third world war but the truth is that the way the conflict has been stoked corresponds with what Pike wrote in 1871:

...The Third World War should be incited taking advantage of the seeds planted by the Illuminati agents to provoke differences between political Zionism and the leaders of the Muslim world. The war should be channelled in a way that Islam and Zionism destroy each other and that other nations will involve themselves too to the extent that they become physically, mentally, spiritually and economically exhausted...

Without the benefit of hindsight, it would be possible for us to think that these are just fantasies made up by people who get a thrill from messianic or prophetic conspiracies. But when the content of the letter talks about First, Second and Third World Wars, and if we take into consideration that it was written in the 19th-century, it is difficult not to be amazed. Regarding the description in the texts about the third world conflict, it is worth noticing that after 11 September 2001 in New York and the Madrid bombings of 11 March 2004, Bin Laden and Al Qaeda could be taken to represent the Muslim world as described in Pike's letter. The Israel-Palestine conflict is still unresolved, and there are no signs of resolution in the near future.

There is something else that is also worth highlighting. Pike says in his letter 'that other nations will involve themselves too to the extent that they become physically, mentally, spiritually and economically exhausted'. A year after the Gulf War, the voices speaking out against it came not only from the US but also from other traditionally allied nations. Working alongside them, Islamic terrorism became stronger and more established.

At the time of writing this book, the first Islamic terrorist attack against the so-called political Zionism has just occurred. It happened in

Photograph of 11 September 2001. One of the Twin Towers before its collapse

Egypt, but in an area that borders Israel and one that is commonly frequented by the Israelis: the East of the Sinai Peninsula.

It is frightening to think that these relatively modern conflicts may have been planned at the end of the 19th century, by conspirators seeking worldwide chaos, as suggested in *Angels and Demons*.

6. How Naïve to Believe We Are Free

He who renounces himself in the name of God, has killed
his true self:he is the living dead. His existence will be an eternal
flight from the only reality that could ever be.

Ortega Y Gasset

The Illuminati officially disappeared from history in the 18th century after the Order apparently disintegrated. Nevertheless, and as if by magic, they reappeared, dotted around the globe with links to secret societies involved in all sorts of affairs. How was it resurrected? Who were the successors?

The development of Illuminati groups has had many ramifications. Some participated directly in the birth of the Communist League and ended up joining the First International. The others, preferring a more contemplative life, like Rudolf von Sebottendorf, were more inclined to follow spiritual activities and founded several esoteric secret societies. One of these was the Thule Group, created in the 1920s. When this society was in its infancy the minutes' secretary was a character who would later instil fear into hearts all round the world: his name was Adolf Hitler.

THE THULE GROUP

In 1918, when after its defeat, German society was highly influenced by occultism, the Thule group was created, inspired by Rudolf von Sebottendorff, an occultist who employed a variety of pseudonyms for different activities. He assumed the alias Rosenkreutz, the name of the official founder of the Rosicrucians, when co-ordinating the secret society called Red Moon. He studied astrology, symbolism, Kabbala and occultism. He is also thought to be responsible for the obscure philosophy of the Nazi ideology.

The name of this new secret society is derived from the legendary kingdom of Thule, thought by some to have been the lost Atlantis. Its values were anti-Semitic and its membership included Adolf Hitler and his lieutenant Rudolf Hess. Its coat of arms was a swastika placed behind a shiny vertical sword representing the power of transmutation and the overthrow of the established powers.

A year after the establishment of the secret society of Thule, one of its members, Karl Hausofer, created a secret order to run alongside Thule called the 'Luminous Lodge'. Its objective was to increase their mysterious and magical knowledge. Hausofer maintained relationships with different mystic groups and held an influence over both the Thule group and the Nazi Party. In fact he is the one thought to have introduced group and the Nazi Party. In fact he is the one thought to have introduced the idea of a new Germany based on purity of race and on the old tradition of the occult practised before Christianity.

P2: THE POWER OF NEOFASCISM

Previous chapters have discussed the aims of the world wars, whether or not they were orchestrated by secret societies. This chapter progresses to a time when peace was restored. It has already been discussed that Giuseppe Mazzini was an Illuminati conspirator and Freemason. However, his role does not end with a conspiratorial correspondence with Pike. Mazzini was the founder of Propaganda 1, a secret group said to be linked to political revolutionary trends that also practised esoteric initiation rites. An even more dangerous Lodge would later emerge from it, P2 or Propaganda Due. This group has been accused of carrying out numerous terrorist attacks, of infiltrating themselves in the Holy See, and according to conspiracy theorists, of plotting and perpetrating the assassination of Pope John Paul I (see Part II).

Poster of the Thule Group, a swastika can be seen behind a vertical sword

After the Second World War, neo-fascist movements were hidden, disguised as national fronts that would later try to blend into democratic political parties without losing their fascist principles. In fact in the 1950s, Italy faced a constant political conspiratorial atmosphere that would continue later in 1964 and 1970 with two specific attempts to overthrow parliament, both attributed to students with a political message. However, from 1977 things began to change and the constant insurgency resulted in the creation of more far-right radical groups. As a result 'Terza Posizione' (Third Position) and 'Nucli Armati Rivoluzionari' (Armed Revolutionary Anits) were founded in 1979. These appeared to be groups of Nazi ideologist students, but in fact there were a number of shadowy societies in the background running these groups. In those shadows, among those secret societies, were the Illuminati.

In the 1980s, taking advantage of an atmosphere that had already been created, P2 decided to take action. On 2 August 1980, 85 people died

Licio Gelli, founder of the Masonic Lodge P2, whose aim was to create a new political order in Italy.

and 200 were injured in a terrorist attack at the railway station in Bologna. In December 1984 there was another attack, this time on the Rome-Milan Express with a total of 16 people killed. The investigators concluded that the secret services were implicated in these attacks and that the conspiracy was the work of a lodge with supposedly Masonic roots. Its name was 'Propaganda Due' (P2), its founder: Licio Gelli, its mission: to overthrow the established leaders of the Italian Republic.

From the 1970s P2 had been focusing on destabilizing national politics through terrorist attacks, with the aim of building their blueprint 'New Order' – but of the Italian state, not of the world. The sinister lodge was run by someone who left nothing to chance. Licio Gelli had many influential friends in the Vatican who facilitated his use of the Church structure to carry out his plans. He had excellent contacts, not only in the Church but with intelligence groups as well. In fact, it has been alleged that he was a double-agent of the CIA and the KGB.

THE BIZARRE CASE OF THE BANCO AMBROSIANO

One of the stories that had a major impact on the public during the 1980s, in which the Church was found to be involved, was the fake bankruptcy of the Banco Ambrosiano of Milan.

Apparently $1,200 million 'disappeared' from this bank. The president of the bank, Roberto Calvi, who had links to the Freemasons and the Illuminati, and the then archbishop Paul Marcinkus, who was the president of the Vatican Bank, better known as the IOR, the 'Institute for Religious Works', were responsible for the scheme.

Conspiracy theorists make a point of this to prove that the hatred between the Illuminati and the Church is still alive today: Marcinkus had the support of the Church and the Papacy, which saved him at the Banco Ambrosiano trials. On the other hand Gelli, who advised on the transactions to beget the bogus bankruptcy, was condemned to twelve years in prison.

Gelli was able to convince and captivate more than one person in power. After P2 was disbanded, investigators found among its members numerous officials from the Vatican and the Italian Armed Forces, including 30 generals and 8 admirals. But there is even more, the secret services chief and a number of businessmen in the media also belonged to the lodge.

The Italian parliament dissolved Gelli's conspiratorial lodge. After the P2's 'official dismemberment', its founder was accused of several crimes but acquitted of them all, at trials at the end of the 1990s he was finally exonerated of all conspiratorial crimes against the Italian state. Was he really innocent or were his influential friends so powerful they were able to free him from any accusations? Perhaps one day history will reveal the truth.

THE NEW WORLD ORDER

The idea of a 'new world order' is a common one. Although the phrase has been attributed to George Bush, Sn, it is not really his. One must not forget that a very similar Masonic-Illuminati symbol had already appeared on the dollar. But if we are looking for more contemporary references let us take the example of Nelson Rockefeller, who, in 1968 after joining the Republican Party and becoming their candidate for that year's elections, said that if he became president he would work as hard as possible to 'create a new world order'. Nelson Rockefeller was a Freemason. The conspiracy theorists have evidence that he was surrounded by advisors linked to the Illuminati, the Grand Lodge Rockefeller and the Order of Skulls and Bones which has some links to the Bush family.

With reference to the conflict between the Church and the Illuminati described in *Angels and Demons*, it is interesting that, in August 1969 when Rockefeller was on his way back from a trip to Latin America, he sent President Nixon a report in which he said: 'the Catholic Church has stopped being one of our trusted allies and

George Bush, Snr, member of one of the most politically influential families in the US and linked to the Order of Skulls and Bones.

a guarantee of social stability in the South American continent... We should study the need to substitute the Catholics with other Christians in South America with the support of fundamentalist groups...'

THE FINANCIAL COVER UP

There are a large number of institutions funded by the richest people in the world with powerful members continuously striving for a new era of global rule. What is known today about these groups is that they are financial or business associations that advise a large number of countries on how to direct their foreign affairs. But things seem to run even deeper than that. Although one could not say that these institutions are ruling the world, one could say they are being used as a cover-up by some members who are indeed commanding the situation.

Consider the following institutions:

THE BILDERBERG CLUB

It is widely considered to be one of the clubs that own the world. Its activities are little known because they are not made public. The Club is formed by country leaders, bankers, global corporation chief executive officers and media magnates etc, and meets in secret just days before the G8, a meeting of the richest countries in the world (Germany, Canada, the USA, France, Italy, Japan, the UK and, since 1997, Russia). Many believe that the Bilderberg Club is a secret branch of the G8, and although it looks just like any other club, it must be said, it boasts the most illustrious membership in the world.

The Bilderberg Club was officially founded in May 1954 in Holland, more specifically in Oosterbeek, and takes its name from the hotel where their first meeting was held. Nevertheless, it is believed that it long existed in the shadows, made up of members of other secret societies. Prince Bernhard zu Lippe-Biesterfeld from the Orange-Nassau House, the present-day Dutch monarchy, was its creator. His name was already well-known, not for being founder of this club but because he had been an officer of Hitler's SS and a member of the Nazi party.

Bernhard zu Lippe-Biesterfeld, who already owned speculative foreign exchange businesses during the Nazi era, decided to create an élite club to unite the world's major powers. He realized that power no longer lay just in religion or politics but in the combination of both and in the industrial, economic and financial world. He was the president of this himself, was to enhance relations between the USA and the European continent. He later nominated Alec Douglas Home as his successor.

Home (1903–1995) was a bright British politician member of the House of Commons until 1945. In 1951 he was the Minister of State for Scotland, and in 1955 he was appointed Commonwealth affairs co-ordinator. Finally, he became prime minister on 19 October 1963 for one year. Another interesting point about this character is that, between 1970 and 1974, he was Foreign Secretary whose job it is to control the foreign affairs policy of the United Kingdom.

After Douglas Home, the Club's president was a German politician who fought with the Air Force (Luftwaffe) during the Second World War. His name was Walter Scheel, who in 1953 was elected as a member of the German Parliament, the Bundestag. He was Minister of Economic Co-operation between 1961 and 1966 and on the 1 July 1974 he became Federal president, a post he kept until 1979. Scheel was chief of the Bilderberg Club until 1985 when he was replaced by Eric Roll, president of a renowned banking group, S. E. Warburg. Another notable president was Peter Carington, better known as Lord Carrington, who had been general secretary of NATO and a minister of several British governments. It is evident that the Club members were nothing if not influential and very powerful people. But does this alone mean it was a hotbed of conspiracies?

Bernard zu Lippe-Biestfeld, founder of the Bilderberg Club

Sir Alec Douglas Home (cover of *Time* magazine, October 1963), successor to Bernard zu Lippe-Biestfeld as head of the Bilderberg Club

There is a curious phrase that says everything about the Bilderberg Club: 'He who manages to enlist, will be promoted shortly after'. This political and social promotion is on an international level and only if the

Walter Scheel, President of the Bilderberg Club and successor to Sir Alec Douglas Home

political and social promotion is on an international level and only if the 'wise advice' from the dominant members of the Club is heeded. Clinton and Blair are very clear examples of this. They joined the Club just before becoming president and prime minister of their respective countries.

The Club, like any other prestigious secret society, does not advertise for members. It is not easy to join this institution. The Club, like the Illuminati, chooses the candidates and not the other way round. The selection process is supposedly based on the specific interest that the Club has in what the candidate is doing at a global level. A committee selects one hundred candidates, who are invited to attend the next voting session. Naturally the candidates must keep this invitation secret: this is essential if they want to maintain a good relationship with a club that also has the collaboration of the CIA and the Israeli secret service, Mossad.

Why so secretive? No one knows when they meet. There are no press conferences or official statements. At the meetings, political and of course financial issues are discussed. One could say that the new world order idea is alive at these meetings. One would assume that considering the globally high profile of attendees, it would be quite normal for the press to be present, but it is surrounded by complete silence and total secrecy.

Not many members have discussed the mechanics of the Club but they have said that 'once there, they are stripped of any authority', i.e. they participate as individuals and leave all of their power at the door. To what extent can all these head of states, tycoons and directors of media empires and global banks remain neutral when they return to their countries? Everything points to the idea that they leave with a particular point of view and with very clear instructions. If in doubt, a call to the Club will suffice.

The media has occasionally spilled the beans and publicized the 'wise advice' given by the Club. For example, they were accused of the Russian bombing in Chechnya. Apparently NATO members of the Club had a secret meeting with President Putin to authorize him to bomb the rebellious region. There is another rumour regarding the Club's role in the end of Margaret Thatcher's career because of her radical opposition to the Euro.

The Club's advice is not always taken. In 2003 the leaked out that Donald Rumsfeld, the US Secretary of Defense and one of the most regular attendees of Club meetings, said after the attack on the Twin Towers that he would not invade Iraq. Nevertheless, as we know, he did. This created a very bad atmosphere in the Club to the extent that Colin Powell had to explain about the military operations of the war in Iraq to Club members.

Many influential journalists have also been linked to the Club, directors of the major newspapers in the US, for example, *The Washington Post*, *The Wall Street Journal*, or the UK's *Financial Times*, and the French *Le Figaro* as well as other European press magnates.

Margaret Thatcher at a NATO meeting in Brussels on 29th November 1977. Her political career as Prime Minister is rumoured to have come to an end following a decision made by the Bilderberg Club

---

SIGNIFICANT CLUB MEMBERS

Although membership of the Bilderberg Club is a secret, names of 'supposed' members are occasionally leaked:

• Alan Greenspan, Governor of the Federal Reserve Bank, closely linked to Nixon and Reagan.
• Henry Kissinger, accused on numerous occasions of being responsible for supporting Pinochet's coup d'état in Chile.
• David Rockefeller, founder of the powerful Trilateral Commission.
• Tony Blair, British Prime Minister, promoter of the 'third way' which proposes solutions to 21st-century issues.
• Bill Clinton, ex-president who tried to turn around politics in the US with a more liberal and humanitarian approach.
• Valery Giscard d'Estaing, ex-president of France who encouraged the relationship with the Third World and the integration of Europe.

THE TRILATERAL COMMISSION: DISCREET BUT NO SECRET?

If the Bilderberg Club is suspected of controlling the world's destiny, another organization, called the Trilateral Commission, founded by one of the members of the Club, is equally worthy of suspicion. In 1973 the global economic community received rather interesting news: the Rockefeller family had decided to create the Trilateral Commission, a club that would be made up of the political and economical élite of the world.

David Rockefeller had a very clear objective for this organization: it had to be selective and only the élite would be able to join. The aim was to create a private establishment that would unite the efforts of the United States, Europe and Japan in all matters political and social in order to control the world's destiny without the problem of territorial boundaries and their governments. Curiously this is very similar to the founder of the Illuminati's hopes for achievement: a global government with power over individual states. During the 1970s it was finance not politics that pulled the strings.

The Trilateral Commission was the way to break with the traditional established power, to take away autonomy and to create a first world front to control the destiny of the second and the third world.

In the Trilateral there was no place for Central and South America, for Africa, nor for any Asian country except Japan. In its initial foundations it is stated:

This commission is created with the aim of analysing the main issues that the United States, Western Europe (the fall of the Wall in Berlin had not

happened yet and Perestroika was quite far away) and Japan have to face. The members of the Commission are very distinguished citizens from these three regions and who have commitments in different areas.

David Rockefeller, founder of the Trilateral Commission

Its way of functioning is very similar to that of the Bilderberg Club: the Trilateral Commission works with absolute discretion; members do not give press conferences and are not permitted to give interviews regarding what goes on in meetings. However they do publish some official reports, undoubtedly censored, on different issues discussed in their meetings. These

From left to right, starting at the top: Colin Powell, George W. Bush, Dick Cheney and Donald Rumsfeld.

reports are written by teams of experts who tell the world 'what should be done leaving national sovereignty and territorial boundaries to one side'. In fact, one aim of the Trilateral is to 'properly manage a global government'.

It is also important to stress that the Trilateral Commission would like to put a new world order in place. This phrase or slogan recurs throughout this book, it is omnipresent when discussing secret societies.

To achieve this new order the members of the Trilateral do not hesitate to make statements and advise governments and global institutions on globalization, free-market economics or financial dealings between the rich and the poor countries, etc. The members of the Trilateral maintain that their position is 'far beyond the established powers' claiming to be 'in a better position to plan and build the world's architecture'.

After 11 September 2001 the Trilateral Commission insisted on the necessity for a new international order and on a global response. Not long after President Bush proclaimed himself as the universal champion of democracy to fight against terrorism anywhere in the world. The US then declared war on terrorism and the 'clean-up' started in Afghanistan. The excuse was to hunt Osama Bin Laden, who was on the run. It is said that the hunt enabled the US to create a new government in Afghanistan on their own terms.

Present at that Trilateral Commission meeting were, among others, Colin Powell, the Secretary of State; Donald Rumsfeld, Secretary of Defense; and Dick Cheney, Vice-President. Some time after, while the US military were still in Afghanistan, they turned to Iraq and the trio said they had proof that Sadam Hussein's government was in possession of weapons of mass destruction. The war on Iraq ensued. New world order and global justice were unstoppable. What will happen next when the re-election of Bush allows them continue and expand their policies?

Compared to other organizations, the Trilateral Commission is more discreet than secretive. From the outside they seem to be above esoteric beliefs and global conspiracy theories. It is an institution known worldwide as a 'board of wise and experienced people'. However, many see through the 'kind' public front of the Trilateral Commission and glimpse other groups behind it, like the Bilderberg Club or even spheres of influence linked to secret societies like the Illuminati and the Freemasons.

PERILOUS GLOBALIZATION

In today's world, globalization is the norm and everything is at our fingertips. States and their frontiers still exist but, is this, in effect, a mirage? In fact, a cold look at the main 'clubs' shows that divorced from the states, flags and frontiers there seems to be a destiny chosen by their leaders and those who meet within what look like innocent organizations and who look at things outside the authority of the national governments.

The secret societies, the real rulers of the world, have tentacles reaching all four corners. The world has become smaller with the popularity of the Internet and access to satellite TV. There are more resources available to us and we have greater access to information than our parents and grandparents. Nevertheless, these advantages are not one-way traffic. In other words, to believe that we are more free now because we have access to information is a mistake.

It works both ways. As well as secret societies, the security services and the governments themselves use technology to maintain control. They can spy using innocent tools such as bank accounts or credit cards; it can be done through internet servers and all the sub-programmes from ISPs in personal computers. Those pulling the strings in the shadows have the capacity to find out when you go online; the kind of browsing you do; which electronic publications, of what political slant, you read. They can find out your musical, political, social and even your sexual inclinations.Today, four innocent mouse clicks can give away everything about our lifestyle.

If you think such internet surveillance is ruthless it is nothing compared to other methodologies that are increasingly being used. Do you think that your National Insurance data really go only to the Inland Revenue? Who else might find them useful? How much can the daily use of your credit card say about you? How many times in one day can your mobile telephone signal be detected by a satellite with only a metre's margin of error?

PROPHESIES FOR THE PRESENT

The search for a new world order is not new, it has appeared at different times announced by heads of state of all tendencies:

'National Socialism will make use of its own revolution to establish a new world order' Adolf Hitler
'When peace arrives it will be the time to achieve a new world order' Edward VIII
'I will work for the creation of a new world order' Nelson Rockfeller
'The relationship between the United States and other peoples will be guided by our will to build a new world order' Jimmy Carter
'A new alliance of nations has started… When we win, and we will, we will have a real opportunity in this new world order' George Bush, Snr

Nowadays, we can easily buy ultra-sensitive microphones to listen to the conversations of our neighbours. If this is available at such a small price just imagine what kind of technology can be acquired for those purposes with a government's budget, or by international financial groups.

To believe we are free is paradoxical. Anyone in the totally misnamed Third World has more freedom than us. Conversations are not as easily overheard. What they do in their houses is not likely to be captured by an apparent heating emissions detector placed in the roof of an innocent office building, whose very attractive chimney is, in reality, an antenna. Cities in the First World are full of these works of art.

You can be sure of one thing: Orwell's 'Big Brother' is not just a TV programme but the reality in which we are living.

LUCIFER, THE NEW REDEEMER?

The aim of the Illuminati, as indicated, was to conquer the world after three great wars. Two have already taken place. To initiate the third of the 'cruel battles' would have to be provoked. Could that mean terrorist attacks? After the third war, according to the Illuminati's aims, Christianity would have to be destroyed and this is the object of the plot in *Angels and Demons*. After such upheaval there would be a time for redemption and a new era of the 'Illumination of the minds'. It would be the time for Lucifer who, according to the Illuminati, is not the demonic figure described by the Church, but a symbol of elevation. The Illuminati see Lucifer as the real carrier of 'The Light'.

The scheme, despite the many events we have already mentioned, has only just begun. As the next chapters will show, the secret societies have woven a delicate web to give them control over humanity in the next few centuries. There are extremely telling inclusions in the documentation belonging to the Illuminati:

We will expel the nihilists and the atheists and we will provoke social chaos that in all its horror will very clearly show to all nations the effect of absolute atheism, which is the savage perpetrator of the cruellest of actions. Then the people, feeling forced to defend themselves against the revolutionary minority, will exterminate the destroyers of civilization.

The masses will grow disappointed with Christianity, they will lack direction or leadership and will be anxious to find an ideal. Unsure where to focus their adoration they will receive the true light through the universal manifestation of Lucifer's pure doctrine at last uncovered for everyone to see, manifestation that will continue with the destruction of

Christianity and atheism, both simultaneously conquered and then destroyed...

Secret societies seem to be more powerful than God and divinity. The global conspiracy groups exist and work everywhere. The have their own temples, rituals and ceremonies. They are growing thanks to people's disbelief in their existence. They are ignored; no one cares about the disconcerting things said about conspiracy groups. It seems as if they are saved by their own esoteric image which simply makes them look like groups of eccentrics. Nevertheless, everything points to the fact that the world is under the rule of a powerful and invisible global government whose aim is to follow, feed and keep alive the ideology of an ex-German Jesuit called Adam Weishaupt, founder of the Illuminati. The 'Devil's Chapels', the archetype which we shall use to illustrate the Illuminati's aims, are practically everywhere, and some even say they have gone so far as to influence the Church. Some investigators have gone even further, claiming that the Illuminati are already entrenched in the Vatican.

In his novel *1984*, George Orwell foresaw a global society where tight control would be executed over each individual, anticipating surveillance methods used in western societies

91

IN BIG BROTHER'S HANDS

Things can even go beyond that. In theory, the Trilateral Commission is composed of groups representing the highest profile individuals in business, finance and politics in the USA, Europe and Japan. Up to this point, all may seem well but it is not common knowledge that the Trilateral Commission promotes links and collaboration with the Freemasons. What has also not been officially recognized is that the Illuminati are standing close behind the Freemasons.

Conspiracy theorists say that the so-called new world order follows the practice of the favourite Illuminati symbol: the pyramid represented on the dollar bill. It is worth mentioning here that President Washington was a Freemason, as was his rival, Thomas Jefferson.

Conspiracy theorists say that the members of the Bilderberg Club, founded in 1954 and comprising the 500 most influential individuals in the world, are at the base of that pyramid. Above them is the so-called 'Supreme Council of 33', formed by the highest-ranking Freemasons in the whole world. Above these Freemasons is the Council of the 13 Great Druids. Above is 'The Tribunal', consisting of unknown individuals. The most striking is the top of the pyramid. All councils, boards and estates are ruled by a person with the seventy-second grade of Kabbala practitioners. This individual receives the title of: 'The Illuminatus', the all-powerful big brother brought forth from the darkness by Weishaupt and reintroduced in 1949 by George Orwell in his prophetic novel *1984*.

On 1 August 1972 one of the representatives of the pyramid sent out a cryptic phrase, that many people were willing to link with the fall of the Twin Towers: 'The day the lights in New York go out, you will know our objective has been achieved'. Were the World Trade Center Towers the lighthouse or the torch that marked global change?

PART 2

THE
DESTRUCTION
OF THE CHURCH

7. Secret Plots inside the Church

The Catholic Church has always refused to comment officially on stories about sects or secret societies despite, as we have seen in the first part of this book, many of these secret societies having aims of destroying the Papacy. Nevertheless the Papacy has been home to the development of 'orders' similar to secret societies because of their clandestine nature, and their organization and hierarchy. These societies have submitted to the power of the Church and have been a very important tool for it.

To understand what seems like a contradiction, one must not forget that the Church itself was initially a persecuted secret society and that it has never been very fond of revealing its internal affairs. Its origins, miracles, secret plots and conspiracies are as numerous as the number of books, articles and films it has inspired. It is therefore unsurprising that the plot in a fictional book like *Angels and Demons* is inspired by the complicated and dark network that is the Vatican.

The portrayal of the Vatican and Rome is one of strange concepts, peculiar rituals, picturesque characters and locations that could have been plucked from a film. What is behind the fiction in *Angels and Demons*: What is the role of the Institute for Religious Works? How is a conclave conducted? Is there a guiding hand in the shadows behind the senior official posts? Who manages the Vatican funds? Does the Pope really have any power?

A fair amount of the goings-on behind the secret societies has been discussed, including their conspiracies. It is now time to look closely, not only at the institution that the novel bases itself upon, but also at where most of the action takes place.

A DEEP-ROOTED UNIVERSAL POWER

The Apostolic Roman Catholic Church is the most consistently powerful existing institution in history. For two millennia it has directed, influenced and been at the centre of the main developments in the West and most of the world. Since its beginning it has spread through Europe, Africa, America, the Far East and the islands of Oceania. It has witnessed the fall of absolutist monarchies, the accession of democracy, capitalism, communism and the arrival of globalization in the 21st century of its reign.

There is no other powerful institution, either spiritual or secular, that has survived as long as the Catholic Church and part of its secret has been not to change its hierarchical structure. To deal with new events without damaging that resilient hierarchy, other parallel structures have

The Vatican has been a hive of 'orders' similar in nature to secret societies
in terms of its operations, organization, secrecy and hierarchy

been put in place to carry out specific tasks as directed. Many, like the Order of the Knights Templar, were disposed of when their usefulness ceased or when they became a threat to the Pope's power. Others, like the Jesuits, have served their purpose introducing reforms without changing, at least in appearance, the principles of the doctrine. These 'parallel branches' have also served the purpose of bringing together all the dissenting voices, using dialogue to restore unity.

The main difference between the sects or external secret societies and the religious orders is that the latter have been conceived inside the Church. Their subsequent development may have separated them from canonical doctrine, but they have very rarely been able to cut their umbilical link with the Church. Therefore, their relationship with the Vatican is very different from that of secret societies. Although secret societies may have been able to infiltrate the Church's structure at some point, they were not created there, at least not officially.

To develop this argument the we will look at the three most representative societies or ecclesiastic orders that developed within the Church: the Knights Templar, the Jesuits and Opus Dei. These are three very different examples to demonstrate the different detours taken by the Church to maintain its power.

THE KNIGHTS TEMPLAR: GUARDIANS OF CHRIST'S HERITAGE

The origins of the Order of the Knights Templar are lost in the mists of time. There are many tales about an ancient mission rooted in their legacy before being established inside the Catholic Church. Some believe they are Atlantis' survivors, others that they are descendants of the old Celtic Druids. They have also been linked to Christian esoteric cults, more specifically Christological, or to some Islamic secret societies with whom they mixed during the Crusades.

It is very probable that the Order of the Temple was created by Robert de Molesmes, a Benedictine monk who, in 1098, founded the Cistercian order. The monks of this order followed a very strict vow of poverty, even in their forms of worship and any kind of research or reading that might be blasphemous was prohibited. Saint Stephen Harding introduced a strict set of rules in his 'Charter of Charity' and in the text *De Laude Novoe Militae* of Saint Bernard of Claraval. In this work, this Cistercian monk of noble origin explained his idealist view of the Christian Knightly orders, which he called God's militia. This was a very common concept at the times, combining the role of a monk with that of a knight, creating a dual character who prayed in times of peace and fought in times of war when it was necessary to defend (or impose) the Christian faith. The Knights Templar and other knightly orders gained power since they were active in the three strategic areas that dominated the medieval world: religion, politics and the military.

The official creation of the Order of the Knights Templar was in 1119 in the Holy Land, after the first Crusade. The Christian forces had regained Jerusalem and its temple, but their position was precarious and they were nearly totally surrounded by Muslims. The threat was not only to the newly conquered city but to the roads that lead to it. This is why Hugo de Payns, from Champagne, and eight other French Knights decided to form a group that would protect the pilgrims and take custody of the Holy sites. Pope Baldwin II of Jerusalem assigned them a building next to the temple as their headquarters. They lived in spartan conditions and were thus dubbed the 'pauvres chevaliers du temple', which is how they acquired their name.

Hugo de Payns had taken the initiative but he also knew that without the approval of the Pope they would be a sect without resources. He also knew that such a movement must have more than its nine volunteers and therefore decided to make it into a knights' order. To be able to do this he had to go to Rome to get the Pope's approval. He did this through the Council of Troyes (1128). It was agreed that the Knights Templar would abide by the Benedictine Order, as well as taking three vows for life and following exceptionally severe living rules.

Despite the harshness of the rule there were many volunteers. There are several theories as to why. Some believe people joined because they thought that the Knights Templar possessed secret magic powers.

Saint Robert, Saint Alberic and Saint Stephen Harding, three of the founders of the Cistercian Order

Others thought it was simply the best route for a knight looking for action in times of peace to take. The large numbers of applicants forced the Order to establish a hierarchy, which was curiously similar to that of the Islamic Assassins (see Appendix 1, p. 137). The fraternity was organized into four ranks: knights (the warriors), squires (light cavalry), farmers and chaplains. The last two groups did not have to fight. To show their adherence to the Order they wore the white Cistercian habit with a red cross on the chest.

Apparition of the Virgin to Saint Bernard of Claraval (oil painting by Fra Filippo Lippi)

The Order of the Knights Templar grew for nearly two centuries, and had a very good reputation amongst the European monarchs and the Church. Both rewarded the Order with land, castles and tax exemptions, which made them envied by the other hangers-on. The Knights Templar acquired great independence because they were settled in far-away lands and they gradually became more independent until little by little, they drifted away from the dictates of the Vatican.

AN EXEMPLARY TEMPLAR

The Knights Templar set an example of bravery in battle and of piety in the monasteries. In fact, their numbers were less important than the example they set to the rest of the Christian knights. It is believed that at their height there were approximately 400 knights alone in the Order, a modest number but with disproportionate power, not just in the world of knights but also gained through the wars. Furthermore, when captured, they never renounced their faith (the only means of escaping death offered to them by the Muslims). It is believed that in two centuries 20,000 Templar knights and squires died.

In a bid to enlarge their ranks, the Templars had to be more open regarding recruitment and thus had to slacken their strict entrance requirements. In the end, to gain membership, one had only to pass a secret test. This is still secret today and there is a good deal of speculation about what it involved. The order became very wealthy (it is believed that they owned approximately 900 properties) which corrupted their noble values. The other orders disapproved of their wealth, pride and passion for power. The Order of the Knights Hospitalier, which had been created following the example of the Order of the Temple, was one of their most tenacious rivals. These internal rivalries and tensions could have worked in favour of the Muslims, and finally in 1187, Saladin and his army expelled the Christians from Jerusalem.

Towards the end of the 12th century the Church found the schemes and plots between the Templar and the Hospitalier so unbearable that a number of successive Popes thought it best to merge the two orders. Saint Louis officially proposed it at the Council of Lyon (1274) and Pope Nicholas IV proposed it again in 1293. Both orders ignored these recommendations. Things had already heated up when Phillip IV, nicknamed Philip the Fair, condemned the Order of the Knights Templar. The monarch wanted to use their wealth to finance a new crusade but it was difficult to go against an institution backed by the Church. Nevertheless, he convinced Pope Clement V, known for his weak character, to condemn the Order. The 'inquisition-style' trial started in 1307 and the accusations were based on gossip surrounding the 'demonic' nature of the Temple: their initiation ceremony was said to be a mysterious pagan ritual, they denied Christ and spat on the cross, they worshipped idols and they tolerated sodomy, as well as a long list of other accusations as scandalous as they were improbable.

The leaders of the Templars were arrested on 13 October 1307, and under torture confessed to all the crimes of which they were accused. The Great Master Jacques de Molay and the other leaders of the Order

Knight Templar leaving the castle for the battleground (miniature from the 13th century)

were burned at the stake and the Order was disbanded. None of the subsequent Popes refounded the Templar Order but according to some researchers it is still alive and operates as a secret society. According to these beliefs the Templars continue to this day with their traditional businesses of banking and insurance. Many of these businesses have to shield the names of their board of shareholders. The business must always be lawful and have legitimate purposes. It is believed that the Order today has 15,000 members, 30% of whom are women. Their influence covers more than twenty countries, above all the United States, Latin America, the Middle East and Southern Europe. Their members live an austere life and any profits made must go to charity. There

Jacques de Molay, last of the Great Masters of the Temple, burned to death, accused of heresy, in Paris, 19 March 1313

have been rumours for some time regarding a possible approach by Temple to the Vatican, in order finally to obtain pardon for the Order.

THE POWERFUL SOCIETY OF JESUS

The Society of Jesus officially began in 1540 with Paul II's Papal bull, *Regiminis Militantis Ecclesiae*. There is no doubt that the Society was created as a tool for the Church to keep its power.

Christian traditions had become rather lax, which led to widespread discontent and scepticism amongst its followers. Calvin and Luther reflected this feeling when the Reformation was declared, and different 'protestant' worships branched out in Northern Europe and began spreading into Latin kingdoms traditionally faithful to the Vatican. Their reaction was the Counter-Reformation, a movement that exalted liturgy and Catholic symbolism and at the same time tried to solve the Church's internal problems. But, because the counter-attack had to fight on all sides, an Order was created with a new strategy and more flexible tactics: it was

Ignatius Loyola: the enlightened mystic

This Spanish priest was the founder of the Society of Jesus. He was born in 1491 in Loyola, Guipuzcoa. He enrolled to fight alongside the Duke of Najera when still in his teens and during the Revolt of the Communities (1520–1521) suffered a leg wound. While recovering, he read a large number of religious texts that brought him closer to the spiritual life. After staying in seclusion at the Benedictine Monastery of Montserrat he decided in 1522 to live and pray in a cave for ten months, then he left to start his pilgrimage to Jerusalem.

It is worth stressing that until a few years ago a box holding the mat on which Saint Ignatius Loyola meditated and apparently levitated was on display to the public at the Chapel of Palau in Barcelona's old town.

The austerity of his living conditions, his fasting and his profound spirituality made him so light-headed he had frequent visions. Later on, the relation of these episodes made some authors say that he was linked to the Alumbrados who claimed to be enlightened by divine apparitions.

called the Society of Jesus. The founder was Saint Ignatius Loyola – a warlike yet mystic character who imposed these ideals on his congregation, who became known as the 'Soldiers of Jesus'.

The original concept of the Society of Jesus was as a centrally controlled paramilitary organization, but it ended up turning into the intellectual branch of the Counter-Reformation. Their three main objectives were: to update the Catholic Creed from top to bottom, to use education to re-establish the Church's power and to convert the people overseas through missionary work.

Despite the Society's oath of submission to the Pope, as it gradually expanded and got stronger, it acquired a degree of autonomy. Its members devotion to education and science led them to hold very high positions, often in roles that ran counter to Church doctrine, to the extent that the head of the society became known as the 'Black Pope'. However, they ensured there was never an open confrontation with the Vatican and maintained a formal allegiance to the Pope. Some described them as a satanic sect within the Church, and they were expelled from many European countries, including Spain in 1767, in the reign of Carlos III.

Nevertheless, the Society of Jesus has managed to resist the tricks of time and the church hierarchy. The Society has probably contributed more ideas to Christian theology than any other body. Some say it is the most progressive, others that it is simply a mask to maintain and spread the most traditional canonical dogmas. It has also long been the closest Order to the Pope, although in recent years it seems that Opus Dei has taken its place.

OPUS DEI'S VAST SHADOW

It is difficult to explain what the Opus Dei, which in Latin means 'the work of God', really is.

Saint Ignatius Loyola on his death-bed, (anonymous oil painting)

Furthermore, considering that for its followers it is the direct way to sanctity, for its many detractors it is a sect with important connections in the world of political and financial power.

On 6 October 2002, John Paul II canonized Josemaría Escrivá de Balaguer, in front of more than 100,000 Catholics and members of Opus Dei. Very soon afterwards he was made a saint in an unusually short time. The last few years have been very good for Opus Dei. Its growing influence inside the Catholic Church has been unstoppable since John Paul II awarded them with a statute previously sought by its founder for many years: the statute of Personal Prelature. In practice, this means that the organization is managed by a prelate directly named by the Vatican and whose decisions are secret: he only accounts to the Pope. In addition, Opus Dei is completely independent within the Church and is in no way subjected to the jurisdiction of any diocese.

This story begins when Josemaría Escrivá de Balaguer founded Opus Dei on 2nd October 1928. Escrivá wrote a proposal citing Opus Dei as the best way for people of all social backgrounds to find sanctity without retiring from the world, while still able to have a family and a profession. To achieve this they had to strictly follow the outlook of Opus Dei by using a book of rules hand-written by the founder itself: *The Way*. This is the description given by the organization itself: 'The essential quality of Opus Dei is that no one is taken out of their situation, everybody fulfils their tasks and duties in their own status, in the Church's mission, and in civil society, as well as possible'.

Some of the spiritual qualities declared by Opus Dei are to make family and work values sacred, in addition to the love of freedom, prayer and sacrifice, charity, the spreading the word of God, and a pious life.

Josemaría Escrivá de Balaguer, founder of Opus Dei, the order with the greatest influence in the Vatican today

These are Escrivá's words: 'an ordinary life can be sanctified and filled with God' and 'The Lord calls us to sanctify ordinary tasks because Christian perfection can also be found in them'. Therefore, Opus Dei converts the small tasks that fill a regular Christian's life into the sublime: little details like manners, respect for each other, materialistic order, punctuality... 'The greatest sanctity is in the fulfilment of the "small duties" of each moment', concluded Escrivá. And amongst those 'small duties' marriage, fiercely defended by the founder of Opus Dei, has a very important place: 'To a Christian, marriage is not just a social institution or a remedy for human weakness: it is a real spiritual vocation'. With regards to the sanctification of work the following maxim is repeated: 'Sanctify work, sanctify oneself through work, sanctify with work.' One has to accomplish this with as much human perfection as possible (professional competence) and with Christian perfection (for the love of God and to serve humanity).

The spirit of Opus Dei calls upon the cult of prayer and penitence to keep the effort of sanctifying everyday duties alive. This is why members faithfully follow the practice of prayer, reading and study of the Gospel to the letter. But the most faithful also resort to spiked belts and physical self-castigation. They performed these sacrifices to purify themselves of personal sins and as an offering to Christ as repair for all worldly sins.

Regarding their love for freedom, detractors of Opus Dei will only smile in disbelief when they read that 'Opus Dei members are citizens with the same rights and the same obligations as the rest of their fellow men. In all their political, financial, social, etc. activities, they act with full freedom and personal responsibility with no intention of involving the Church or Opus Dei in their decisions; neither do they portray themselves as uniquely able to represent the faith. They respect freedom and the opinion of everyone.'

Charity and the spreading the word of God force the members of the Opus Dei to give testimony of their Christian faith, first by being

Who was Josemaría Escrivá de Balaguer?

Opus Dei was founded in 1928 by Josemaria Escrivá de Balaguer, a 26-year-old priest. Jose María Escrivá Albas (his real name) was born in Barbastro, Huesca, in 1902. In 1940 he asked to be known as Escrivá de Balaguer y Albas; in 1960 he changed from Jose María to Josemaría. During Franco's dictatorship he would to go to the palace of El Pardo to lead religious services for the dictator's family. In 1968 he requested and was awarded the title of Marquis of Peralta. He died in 1975 and Pope John Paul II beatified him in 1992, sanctifying him ten years later.

exemplary and then with the power of word, trying to convince people of the righteousness in following Christ's path. Finally, their ideology advocates that the friendship with God, the daily activities and the personal apostolic determination of each Christian must blend and harmonize with a 'simple and strong way of living', an expression often used by Opus Dei's founder. According to Escrivá: 'A Christian working in this world should not lead a double life, that is to say, a private life – a life for the relationship with God on one side; and a different and separate life on the other side – a social, professional and a family life. One should have only one life, made of flesh and spirit, and this is how it should be – in the soul and in the body – sanctified and filled with God.'

According to data provided by Opus Dei itself, today the organization has 84,000 members worldwide. There are 48,000 in Europe (33,000 in Spain and 4,000 in Italy), 29,000 in America, 4,700 in Asia and Oceania and 1,600 in Africa. Very few of them are priests, scarcely 1,700 in fact, and the rest are members (around 26%) and supernumeraries (approximately 73%). The supernumeraries are men and women, single or married, who give part of their income to Opus Dei.

Having member status implies a special level of commitment; they are the hard-core nucleus of the organization. They live in the Opus' centres but to do so they have to go through a year-long test, sign a permanent contract called 'of fidelity' (equivalent to vows), which includes a pledge of poverty, chastity and obedience. These members usually work in the professional world (being doctors, lawyers, professors, politicians, etc) but donate their whole income to the director of the centre. They make Opus Dei the beneficiary of all their possessions and receive a small wage in return. They are divided into three categories: the voters (those able vote in the election of the new president of the Opus), the enlisted (those in a position of responsibility within the organization) and the ordinary (those who hold managerial posts).

The prelature organizes lessons, talks, outings, spiritual advice etc. for all members as a way of advancing knowledge of the teachings of the Gospel and Church. The training courses – for men and women separately – are organized to be compatible with work and family duties.

But, apart from those who have publicly announced their adherence, members of Opus Dei safeguard their privacy to the full. In article 191 of the charter written in 1950 it says: 'Members and supernumeraries must know that they should always keep a careful silence about the names of other members and that they should never reveal themselves as belonging to the Opus'. This may be the reason why Opus Dei is deemed a secret society. In fact there are some codes that members use. For example, if someone bumps into the Spanish ex-minister Federico Trillo, who has made his membership of Opus Dei public, and salutes him with the Latin word *Pax*, this well-known politician will recognize this person as a member of Opus Dei and will reply with the Latin expression: *In aeternum*. This is the usual way for members of this organization to greet each other. The preservation of privacy is fundamental in the institution's strategy.

While on the subject of ministers, Opus Dei (with bankers, politicians, and businesspeople amongst its members) has been criticized many times for, amongst other things, gathering its members only from an élite group of people who exert an enormous influence over society. In response to this accusation, the members of the prelature answer with the words of Opus Dei's founder that anyone can belong to the Opus, regardless of talent or social status, and that those involved in politics are, independently as free citizens, following their own criteria, and that they do not represent the Opus. Their detractors cynically recall the enthusiastic words of Escriva in the 1960s when Franco included several members of the Opus Dei in his government for the first time: 'We have become ministers!'

The detractors also point the finger at the particular phobia that the Opus has against sex. This is an obsession that at times can become morbid, as is printed in *The Way*: 'Take away from me, Jesus, the rotted crust of corruptive sensuality that obscures my heart.' In fact the current prelate, Javier Echevarría, even said once that when someone is born with a physical disability it is because their parents engaged in the practice of sinful sexual acts. Much has been said about the censorship imposed on members. Opus Dei stoutly denies any kind of censorship but members undergo constant indoctrination courses, and the list of books they can read while they are with the Opus is drawn up by the director of the centres, who then gives them a value from 1 ('recommended') to 6 ('seriously dangerous to the faith').

Regardless of all these accusations directed at the prelature, legitimate or not, the truth is that the Opus has always said that members are there because they wish to be. Once again *The Way* provides the answer: 'To obey is the safe way. To blindly obey a superior is the way to sanctity. To obey your ministry, the only way: because in the work of God, the spirit must learn how to obey or be gone'.

The links between the Church and its own internal secret societies are more than evident. However, it is always a wonder how many of the groups which, at their core, have enjoyed and still do enjoy a certain 'superiority', are waiting for the traditional papacy to come to an end. In the meantime they remain in the shadows…

Some societies' memberships include important political figures. Several politicians from the former Spanish government belong to Opus Dei (left: Romay de Beccaria; bottom left: Federico Trillo; bottom right: Loyola de Palacio)

8. Murder in the Vatican

Angels and Demons tells the story of a plot to destroy of the Church and the Papacy. However, the Pope is not murdered by an external conspiracy; he is poisoned by someone inside the Vatican itself.

Throughout the history of the papacy there have been suspicious deaths that have led to thoughts of a conspiratorial darkness hanging over the Vatican. In this sense a distinction should be made between presumed past assassinations and today's conspiracy theories about the death of John Paul I and the attempt to assassinate John Paul II. Specific cases will duly be investigated, ones that have been conspiracy theorists' favourite subjects in recent years. To better understand these alleged crimes, one must return to the dark deaths of the past and examine how the world functioned at the time.

When the Catholic Church became the majority religion in the West it gained a significant position at the heart of world power. In Medieval times knowledge was kept in the churches and monasteries, safe from the attacks of the Christianized barbarians. During the Renaissance the new concept of the city-state benefited the Church, and its power grew rapidly. It adopted the structure of a conventional state (the Papal States) but had an overarching power over all of them. Intrigues at the Vatican were a thousand times great than any other number of palace intrigues at the time. The Pope, aside from being a spiritual leader, is somehow the most powerful ruler in the whole of Europe. His decisions can start a war, enrich a poor man or impoverish a wealthy one. This leads to a dangerous conflict of earthly and spiritual interests, which in many cases results in the former winning over the latter.

An example of this phenomenon is the stories of corrupted popes, in-house struggles for power at the heart of the Church, and many other chilling events that the Vatican has preferred to keep secret. Amongst all these intrigues, there is also a list of popes wiped from the scene because their reign was not in the interests of certain parties.

'LET US SAY HIS HOLINESS HAS PASSED AWAY'

Before proceeding, some ideas mentioned earlier need clarification. In past times, criminology did not exist and consequently proof of events was scarce, so it is difficult to separate truth from legend and speculation. History books cannot give us a definitive answer about how pope succeeded pope. In addition, we are faced with the Vatican's traditional fondness for secrecy.

Nowadays, one may openly discuss any alleged crime committed in the history of any European court. With the passage of time, forms of government have changed radically and such discussions no longer have the power to harm. Such crimes were occasional lapses that do not affect the country's integrity. But, on reviewing the Vatican's history, such ideas are turned on their head. The Church has altered neither its hierarchy nor the way it functions. So, to admit to past errors would undermine belief in the very system that makes it work. Moreover, this is an organization that managed to become very powerful while it preached (as it still does) virtue and discipline. To accept that crimes, conspiracies and assassinations took place would cast doubts on the validity of the Church, not only in the past but in the present and future as well. This all makes it difficult to discover which popes were actually assassinated during the dark history of the Holy See. There is no convincing proof but there is a suspiciously long list of deaths from non-natural causes. Endeavouring to stick to reliable proof, an attempt will be made to trace the path that will lead to more recent crimes.

The Vatican's corridors have been the setting for many intrigues and conspiracies

THE MARTYR POPES

Several popes died as martyrs when Christianity was suffering persecution from Imperial Rome. Their executioners believed that this would serve as an example to the rest of the Christians. Incidentally, to choose a new pope and rebuild the Church hierarchy was not an easy task, because having to communicate and meet secretly created difficulties. Nevertheless, and even though there were also internal problems, the first Christians managed to preserve the continuity of Saint Peter's throne. Thus the Romans failed in their intention of dealing a knockout blow to Christianity. In fact, Dan Brown uses the same reason in his book: ridding the church of its leader in order to destroy it. However, if this happened, the structure and the power of the Vatican would be very difficult to break.

Saint Peter, the first Pope, was also the first to be executed for his beliefs. Like his master he was crucified, but he asked to be crucified upside down with his head towards the ground considering himself unworthy of the same death as Jesus. Some satanic sects have taken this as a wink of complicity towards their doctrines, given that the inverted cross is the chosen symbol of demonic cults.

Saint Clement I, Saint Peter's successor, suffered the same fate in 97 AD. The sacrament of confirmation and the use of the word 'amen' have been attributed to this early Christian pope. He was exiled by Trajan and later sentenced to death and thrown into the sea with an anchor chained to his neck. Later it was the turn of Calixtus I, who during his reign (217–222) ordered the construction of the catacombs by the Via Appia, where 46 Popes and 200,000 martyrs were buried. In the end, he was caught by the Romans who beat him to death. His body was thrown down a well on the site where the Church of Santa Maria in Trastevere was later erected. The clearest case, which is hardly in any doubt at all, was the assassination of Sixtus II, pope for just a year between 257 and 258. The Church was still being persecuted by the Romans when the Pope and two deacons were found taking refuge in the catacombs. They were ordered to abjure to their Christian faith in order to stay alive; they refused and were beheaded.

The death sentence imposed upon Christians by the Romans was intended as a means of persuasion, but it did not prevent the continuing expansion of the Christian faith. When Christianity eventually triumphed and the persecution stopped, the Church could become settled and establish its hierarchy. From that moment on, presumed assassinations of Popes have resulted from conspiracies, mainly among the Pontiffs' most trusted circle. In other cases, conspiracies have been carried out by enemies feeling threatened or harmed by the Vatican's politics.

CELESTINE V: THE ONLY ABDICATION

Pietro Angeleri, also known as 'Pietro del Morrone', was a Benedictine hermit who in 13th-century Italy was renowned for having attained a degree of sanctity. As mystic as we was coarse, he was snatched from his hermitage in Abruzzi in (1924) to be crowned Pope under the name of Celestine V. The Church had been undergoing a two-year internal power struggle and the conclave of cardinals demanded that the gap be filled with a 'transitional Pope', one who would be weak and submissive until solutions were found. Good old Pietro was the perfect candidate: ignored and ignorant, nearly 90 and with no ambition for power. So he was forced to accept a post for which he considered himself unfit and in which he was never comfortable. One of the few things they allowed him to do was to establish the Celestine Order, which was disolved in the 19th century.

Five months into his Papacy, he realized he was being manipulated by his advisors and that, because of his lack of knowledge and education, he did not know how to behave in the rarified environment of the Vatican. When he realized he was not up to standard he had the decency, and was probably relieved, to resign. He gathered the prelates together and lay face-down on the floor and asked for their forgiveness. After which he announced his abdication and requested permission to return to his life as a

Top right: Celestine V; bottom right: Clement I; bottom left: *The Crucifixion of Saint Peter*

hermit. This gesture has made him the only Pope in the history of the Papacy who has left the position alive.

His successor, the dominant Boniface VIII, to ensure that his opponents would not use the old hermit to question his legitimacy, ordered that he should be taken from his cave and imprisoned. Celestine V died a natural death while in prison. At least this is what the Church claimed and what was believed for nearly seven centuries. In 1988 someone stole the coffin from Pope Angeleri's shrine at the Basilica of Collemaggio, in the region of Aquila; it was later found 60km (40 miles) from its tomb. The Vatican scanned the remains to prove them authentic. A hole, evidently made with a square iron nail, was discovered in his temple. The archbishop of Aquila, Monsignor Mario Peresin, officially confirmed that Celestine had been murdered. And it is not difficult to guess by whom.

THE EXTRAVAGANT AND SUSPICIOUS DEATH
OF THE BORGIA POPE

Rodrigo Borgia was born in Jativa, Valencia, and was better known as 'the Borgia Pope'. He ruled from 1492 to 1503 with the papal name of Alexander VI. He was without doubt the most infamous pope of all times and also the most vilified. During his reign he did his utmost to make his three children (Cesare, Giovanni and Lucrezia) rich. He also behaved outrageously and did not always live within the law. Some historians believe

Portrait of Pope Alexander VI, 16th century. Known as 'the Borgia Pope', he was doubtless the most polemical and criticized Supreme Pontiff in history

the behaviour of the Borgia family was not as extreme as was recorded, rather that it was common at the time for those, including popes, cardinals, bishops and clergymen who could afford to, to conduct themselves in that way. Others believe that his dark reputation was invented by enemies of the Church to discredit the Vatican. Regardless, the excesses of the Borgia Pope seem outrageous by today's standards. The simple fact he had two wives (Vanozza Cattanei and Julia Farnesi) and acknowledged children borne by both is scandalous enough.

Nevertheless, not even his worst enemies could deny that, his extravagant private lifestyle aside, he was a skilled and effective pope who increased and strengthened the power of the Church. When he died in 1506, not before signing the Papal bull *Inter Caetera* that divided the land of the New World between Spain and Portugal, it was a catastrophic blow to the power of the Borgia clan. A large number of historians believe that Alexander VI was poisoned with arsenic. His body swelled and blackened; a fact his enemies claimed showed he was the devil himself. His body swelled much that that gravediggers had to stand on the coffin in order to close it.

It is hard to know with any certainty who might have been responsible for his death in such troubled times, when every king wanted a piece of Italy and there were many among them with reason for wanting to dispose of such an astute and powerful pope.

SIXTUS V, A POPE WITH MANY ENEMIES

Sixtus V, remembered as one of the most energetic popes in history, and who governed between 1585 and 1590, had a tragic end that is still unexplained, but that was possibly the result of some of the controversial decisions he took. He was born in Grottamare in 1520 and baptized as Felipe Peretti. He ascended to Saint Peter's throne after a brilliant ecclesiastic career. Led by his firm and resolute character, in five years his armies had rid the states of bandits, while at the same time increasing papal lands and consolidating his power in Italy.

Sixtus V tried to keep separate the spiritual power of the Church and the worldly power of monarchies, while still being caught up in their quarrels. He supported the Spanish King Philip II in his war against Queen Elizabeth I, because the King and the Vatican had common interests. Philip wanted an end to pirate assaults on his ships and to England's support for the Dutch and Flemish rebels while the Pope wanted to make an example of and punish the Virgin Queen, head of the dissident Anglican Church (founded by her father, Henry VIII). Sixtus V gave the Spanish King some of the funds to create the Armada that would go on a form of crusade against England. After a handful of confrontations with the English, the Duke of Medina Sidonia, the not-very-expert admiral in charge of the Spanish fleet, withdrew without even attempting to disembark. Most of the vessels sank off the Coast of Ireland, as a result of a storm.

After this the Pope decided not to interfere with any secular affairs and used his strong authoritarian will to re-organize the Curia and to take measures in the field of morality. He was the first pope to forbid contraception and abortion, which he deemed as murder, and he condemned the castration of boys to maintain a soprano voice for singing the parts of women in operas. He was a magnificent patron of the arts and commissioned the construction of beautiful buildings and town plans that gave rise to the Baroque splendour of Rome.

Sixtus V died suddenly in 1590, and there is no doubt that he was killed. What is not known is who killed him and which of his controversial measures ignited the rage of those who instigated the crime. According to several studies the Pope was killed by a cleric who was well known to him and who is believed to have lost his mind. Others believe it to be a conspiracy between several governments unhappy with his decisions; or a scheme by prelates displaced from the Curia; it has even been said to be someone who simply hated Baroque art and architecture.

THE MYSTERIOUS DEATH OF CLEMENT VIII

Cardinal Ippolito Aldobrandini became Pope in 1592 when he was 56 and had a great deal of experience of Vatican diplomacy behind him. He was basically a very accomplished negotiator and when he began his reign as Clement VIII he was prepared to show it. He showed great tact and patience in facilitating peace between France and Spain, two favourites of the Church, persuading them to sign the Vervins peace accord in 1598 after decades, even centuries, of animosity. The pact was, however, weak because the French monarch, Henry IV, the Huguenot from Navarre, founder of the Bourbon dynasty, had converted to Catholicism to be accepted as king – the origin of his famous phrase 'Paris is well worth a mass'. However, he later made a pact with the Turks and left the Pope's crusaders high and dry.

Apart from this episode, the most pressing problems that the Pope Clement VIII faced were of a theological kind. He did not hesitate to

Left: coin with the effigy of Clement VIII; Right: coin with the effigy of Sixtus V

confront the respected Spanish Jesuit Luis de Molina. The latter claimed that the free will as defined by the Church did not exist, but was more of a fusion between the will of the individual and divinity. This question, that now seems so irrelevant, created a revolutionary confrontation between the Dominicans and the Jesuits. The Pope gave his support to the former and created a very dangerous enemy in the latter.

Clement VIII died in 1605 in very strange circumstances. Many blamed the Society of Jesus, thought to have killed him to avoid losing influence in the Vatican to the Benedictines. Others maintain, though, that if a crime was committed, the culprit should be looked for among the Calvinist allies of the French King.

PIUS XI AGAINST FASCISM

This vibrant, learned and energetic Pope, who governed between 1922 and 1939 as Pius XI, faced one of the worst periods in Europe and the Vatican. Despite having signed the Lateran Treaty with Mussolini in 1929, an agreement making the Vatican an independent state within Italy, Pius XI never stopped criticizing totalitarian regimes.

Pius XI was did not hesitate to express his opinions, which won him some very fearsome enemies. He was as critical Communism as of Fascism and refused to meet Hitler when the latter visited Rome. The only

Pius XI, Supreme Pontiff before the Second World War, who attempted to prevent what he believed to be an imminent war. He died mysteriously just before releasing an encyclical rigorously criticizing Fascism and anti-Semitism

countries to heed him were those that would later be the 'allies' but at the time their rulers still did not think of Hitler as a menace. When war was about to break out, Pius XI offered his life if it would bring peace. The gesture moved the public but unfortunately not the warring governments.

This brave Pope died in 1939, a day before releasing an encyclical strongly criticizing Fascism and anti-Semitism. The cause of his unexpected death never came to light. Some say that Mussolini gave orders to kill him and that the perpetrator was the Pope's personal doctor who, coincidentally, was the father of the dictator's lover, Claretta Petacci. Whether or not we give any credence to this conspiracy theory, it would not have been very difficult for Doctor Petacci to gain access to the Pope's rooms and inject him with a lethal poison.

JOHN PAUL I: TOO HONEST TO BE POPE

On 29 September1978, at 5 o'clock in the morning, sister Vicenza knocked on the Pope's apartment door but received no reply. As on every other morning the nun was bringing morning coffee to the Pope's office. Concerned by the silence she decided to enter the Pope's room. She found John Paul I had fallen over his desk, dead. Sister Vincenza screamed for the Cardinal Jean Villot, the Vatican's Secretary of State, who just happened to be passing. Villot then called a doctor friend of his, Dr Buzonetti, who issued the death certificate for the Italian citizen Albino Luciani and stated his cause of death as a heart attack. When he announced the death he said, to the horror of Sister Vincenza, that the body of John Paul I had been found by his personal secretary, and not in his office but in his bed.

This was the moment that one of the best kept secrets of the 20th century came into being: that of the brief Papacy of John Paul I and his mysterious death. Albino Luciani had been the head of the Catholic Church for only 33 days, enough time to see that he was about to start a great revolution to restore the Church to the Evangelical message according to the precets of the Second Vatican Council (known as Vatican II). It appeared that the Vatican and its corrupt Curia would be most affected by the drastic reform.

The first thing to raise suspicions of something sinister behind the Pope's death was Cardinal Villot's emphatic refusal for a post mortem to be carried out on the body. Many cardinals had requested this procedure when there was no official report from the doctor and after the Pope's personal physician, Dr Antonio da Ros, expressed his doubts about the cause of death. It is possible that some of the prelates were innocently hoping that a post mortem would halt the gossip, while others wanted to bring to light the crooked political and financial dealings of the secretary of state. Nevertheless, none of them got any satisfaction as Villot, through his aide Cardinal Oddi, declared that the College of Cardinals would not despoil the Pope's remains and would not accept any kind of investigation into the cause of his death.

Dr da Ros did not hide his amazement of the fast diagnosis made by his colleague Dr Buzonetti, who had never treated John Paul I before he signed his death certificate and so was unaware that his medical history included a perfectly healthy heart and a form of a low blood pressure, making a heart attack improbable. Other people close to the late Pope were also surprised as they knew his modest lifestyle, calm character, healthy eating and total rejection of cigarettes and alcohol. Dr da Ros himself had visited Luciani the day before his death and found him in perfect health and with no problems of any kind.

Another concern was that, according to Sister Vincenza, the body was still warm when she found it, making the time of death announced by Dr Buzonetti impossible to believe: 11pm, the previous night. The incorruptible nun dared to tell everything she knew to independent

John Paul I was head of the Catholic Church for 33 days, sufficient to make clear his intent to start a revolution to return the Church back to its Evangelical roots.

informers and investigators, who made her testimony public. Finally, Villot ordered the immediate embalming of the body, which meant all of the internal organs being removed, which in turn meant that there was no way to trace any poison. However, although all fingers pointed to the Secretary of State, it was soon realized that behind it all was an even darker figure: archbishop Paul Marcinkus, director of the Institute for Religious Works, who, despite such a charitable post, managed the financial affairs of the Vatican and not always transparently.

Lately, there have been new voices inside the Church criticizing the amount of missing information regarding the death of John Paul I. Many point to Marcinkus or to his secret and conspiratorial Freemason

Paul Marcinkus: God's banker

Paul Casimir Marcinkus was a priest of Italian origin born in the United States. He was ordained as a priest in Chicago in 1947, and five years later was called to the Vatican. He worked first in the Secretary of State's office, and in 1969, already a bishop, in the Institute of Religious Works, of which he became director two years later. While looking for advantageous investments for the Church he met the banker Michele Sindona, who was laundering money for the Gambino clan, notorious thugs from Chicago. Sindona and Marcinkus started dealing with Licio Gelli, textile magnate and Grand Master of the Propaganda Due (P2) Masonic lodge, who in his youth has belonged to the Nazi SS. The three of them joined forces to carry out financial operations that were as fraudulent as they were secret. Roberto Calvi, a director of the Banco Ambrosiano, then joined them. But after failing in a number of very risky operations, added to the oil crisis of 1972, the arrangement collapsed. Sindona fled to the US, the Vatican lost a fortune and Calvi apparently committed suicide hanging himself from a bridge in London.

Marcinkus denied everything, even his relationship with Sindona. When the prosecutor's office issued an arrest warrant for him, he took refuge in the Vatican City which, as an independent state, was able to reject the extradition warrant.

As it happens, God's banker had made a very large non-recoverable investment to finance the Polish Solidarity movement through the then archbishop Karol Wojtyla, who was elected to the Papacy under the name of John Paul II in 1978, according to some thanks to Marcinkus's threatening and bribing several cardinals. The truth is that the Polish Pope always defended and protected his dubious backer.

Left: Paul Casimir Marcinkus (centre of close-up) in front of John Paul II; right: Michele Sindona

friends. The main prosecution witness is the Cardinal Aloisio Lorscheider, personal friend of the deceased Pope and one of his main supporters of his position. The prelate maintains that Albino Luciani was a very healthy man, who did not suffer from high blood pressure or cholesterol, and who said nothing about a heart problem; hence his extreme surprise when the Pope suffered such a sudden heart attack with no warning. Other civil servants from the Curia have spoken after twenty years of silence adding facts to Lorscheider's testimony. One in particular, the Irish Bishop John Magee, who in 1978 was the private secretary in the Vatican who said at the time that he had found the dead body of the Pope, undoubtedly so that Sister Vincenza would not talk to the press. Magee finally told the truth, including how they moved the body from the office to the bedroom, although he did not talk about it as a crime, nor did he make any accusations.

Such an enigmatic case as the death of a pope in the Vatican attracted the attention of journalists and writers eager to shock the public. Since the beginning and until now there have been more than twenty fiction and non-fiction books published about it, as well as hundreds of articles. Other authors, some of them paid by the Vatican, others members of the Curia, wrote about the case attaching considerable importance to it. On the prosecution side is Roger Peyrefitte with his much researched *La Soutane Rouge*, and the English writer David Yallop, specialist in secret crimes, with the book *In God's Name*, in which he also defends the theory of a Masonic conspiracy. On the side of the defence, John Cornwell, in his book *A Thief in the Night* brilliantly upholds the Vatican's theory, and attacks the figure and reputation of Pope Luciani, asserting that the latter must have kept quiet about his illness, and that this stopped him getting the right medical treatment for the condition.

A SIMPLE BUT FORMIDABLE POPE

John Paul I was a man chosen by consensus because of his righteousness, simple ways and a reputation as a peace-maker. Or at least this is what the cardinals supporting him as a Pope believed. The Conclave of 1978 was torn between two candidates for the papal tiara: Cardinal Giuseppe Siri, who supported the progressive legacy of John XXIII; and the Pole Karol Wojtyla. When both sides realized that they could not obtain a majority of votes, they made a pact to elect the good and honest Cardinal Luciani in the hope of being able to manipulate him.

This man, apparently simple and uncomplicated, was never fully accepted by the Vatican Curia. In his first speech he stated that he preferred to be called spiritual pastor rather than Supreme Pontiff, and with that moment of sincerity and simplicity he had the journalists on side. On another occasion he said, 'God is our Father; even more… our Mother,' which increased the amount of criticism he received in the Vatican and somehow it was justified. The theologians hid their faces in their hands in despair that this Pope would destroy the unalterable dogma of the Holy Trinity. Some of those close to John Paul I said he was shocked when he discovered all the plotting and rivalry in the Vatican. In fact, according to what he said on more than one occasion, he wanted to learn as much as

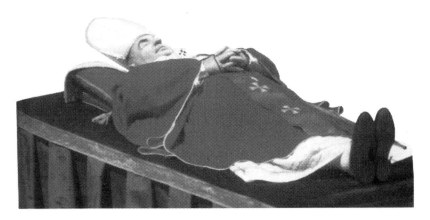

The cause of John Paul I's death remains unknown; rumours point towards members of the Church who were unwilling to accept his intended radical changes, and towards the Masonic Lodge P2

possible about his ministry so that he could reduce his reliance on his advisors, who he thought were too factional and acting out of self-interest. In the opinion of many, John Paul I was too honest to be able to fit in with the Vatican and its schemes, which he also wanted to stamp out.

This attitude created enemies and when there is suspicion of assassination the first step is to investigate the enemies of the victim. According to the writer David Yallop there were at least a dozen influential people who wanted to eliminate the Pope. Among them, of course, is Paul Marcinkus, because the Pope had ordered a detailed investigation into the financial operatioins of the Vatican Bank. Some even say that they saw him around the papal apartment on the day of his death. They saw him a few minutes past five in the morning, the actual time when John Paul I must have died.

According to Yallop, the other suspect was Cardinal Villot, the Secretary of State, who refused to allow a post mortem on the corpse and who manipulated or kept hidden several aspects of the tragic episode. It has been said that the Pope gave him a list of very important names of people to be sacked or transferred. Amongst them was that of Jean Villot himself, who tried to convince the Pope not to carry out such a drastic measure. But John Paul I did not surrender because he knew this step to be crucial to the beginning of his reform. Finally, there is a third suspect, the banker, Licio Gelli who, as discussed, was the leader of the Masonic lodge P2 and who was seriously involved with the financial scandals of Marcinkus and the Banco Ambrosiano.

On the other hand, John Cornwell declares that there was no poison or crime involved but holds the Vatican responsible for letting their leader die. According to his investigations, before he died, the Pope had been complaining for a few days that his legs were swollen and that he had bad circulation. But no one took any notice or asked for the doctor to see him. The official excuse was that the medical report had not yet arrived from Venice, which was Albino Luciano's diocese before he became pope. Negligence or assassination? The question remains unanswered.

It does not matter how you view it, there are too many gaps in the official version. After so many years, the Vatican still has given no evidence to refute such a controversial explanation of the death.

THE CUROIUS ATTACK ON JOHN PAUL II

On the 13 May 1981 the world was shaken by the news that the Pope John Paul II had been the victim of an attempted murder while greeting 10,000 followers in Saint Peter's Square. The young Turkish man Mehmet Ali Agca shot him three times although without aiming correctly. When he tried to escape a French nun threw herself upon him which ensured his detention. Agca nearly ended the Pope's life but did not quite succeed as, after five agonizing hours in the Agostino Gemelli Hospital theatre, the doctors managed to save his life. Some say all the illnesses he suffered after were due to the shooting. Apparently the colon cancer was due to the two bullets that went into his stomach and the wounds to his hand caused his Parkinson's disease. It has also been said that, apart from the physical consequences, the attack also changed his cheerfulness and good humour to a more taciturn manner.

Once again the well-used explanation of the solitary sniper prevailed: he was a mad man who, at his own risk, decided to commit this assassination. However, whoever gave this simple explanation did so to conceal a plot with very specific intentions which was a far cry from the actions of a psychopath.

According to several testimonies, for a long period of time John Paul II was obsessed with finding an answer to this. He closely studied all the articles on the event, as well as reports he obtained from several

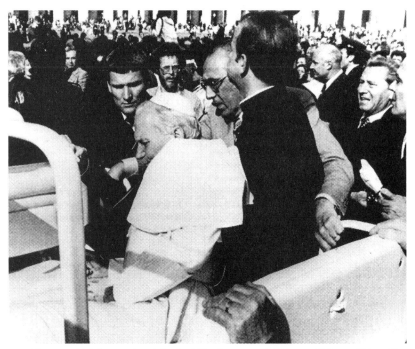

Photograph of the attack on John Paul II by the young Turkish man Mehmet Ali Agca. The motives for the attack have never been sufficiently explained

countries' secret services. The nuncio Luiggi Poggi, dubbed 'the Pope's spy', also made a few inquiries.

On the other hand, the killer received a life sentence and has never provided any concluding evidence on who hired him. It is known that he belonged to a radical organization called 'Grey Wolves'. To some it was a neo-fascist organization, others believe they were radical Muslims and there are those who think that they were Islamic nationalists who were manipulated by the Soviet Union. It appears that Agca, who trained as a terrorist in Syria, had already killed a liberal editor in Turkey in 1979. After that crime he publicly threatened 'John Paul II, head of the crusaders'. Many think that this raving warning brought him to the attention of different groups who could have been interested in killing the Pope. It also seems that he got the Browning gun in Spain and that he was paid $400,000 to do the 'job'.

The election of John Paul II had a special significance for the Polish. The Solidarity movement, led by Catholic trade unionist Lech Walesa, had managed to gain enough support from people in its confrontation of the Soviet government. The Polish Pope was worried that the rash actions of Walesa would provoke a Soviet invasion. It has been said that when the Solidarity leader decided he would organize a massive and aggressive demonstration, Cardinal Stephan Wyszinsky, following the Pope's orders, knelt at Walesa's feet and, holding his legs, said he would not budge until he decided to withdraw the order. Walesa did as the Cardinal said.

The KGB recognized that the Polish question had grown in importance because of the Pope's nationality. Some say that in 1979 the Soviet Communist Party wrote a document recommending the murder of John Paul II. According to some investigators, this letter was signed by Yuri Andropov, the then head of the KGB, and by another high-ranking civil servant in the same institution whose name would become famous worldwide in the ensuing years: Mikhail Gorbachev.

Most intelligence experts believe it was impossible for the KGB to take on such a risky scheme. As they had done many times before, they delegated the operation to their Bulgarian 'sister service', the DS. The DS would have been in charge of the planning and of contacting the killer.

One theory says the murderer was scared that own bosses would kill him, and confessed to the CIA what he was going to do. The American intelligence agency told him to continue with the plan but shooting in the air not aiming at the Pope. This way they would be able to blame the KGB for it. This plan was of no benefit to Ali Agca so he must have decided at the last minute not to go against his bosses and to aim at the Pope.

Many consider that, after the attack, or at least a year later, nearly all intelligence agencies suspected the KGB. It was also common knowledge that there were Soviet spies inside the Vatican. In fact, it seems that the Romanian dictator Ceaucescu told the French secret service about the secret plot and they then informed the Vatican, but no measures were taken to protect John Paul II in the end.

If it is true that everyone knew the KGB was responsible, why not say so publicly? Those who defend this theory say that countries in the West remained silent because Andropov had, in the Kremlin's name, just secretly proposed détente. Unmasking the plot would have meant a step backwards in Cold War issues with an escalation in nuclear weapons. The situation was still very fragile and people were afraid of upsetting the precarious balance.

There is still another theory pointing in a totally different direction. It may not have been communists behind the failed terrorist attack but their future successors and enemy of the West: the radical Islamists, who saw the Pope as the personification of the decadent West and therefore the figurehead that had to be destroyed in order to start his jihad or holy war against the infidels.

Some investigators take the threatening letter sent by Agca to the Pope as proof of this. It said:

The Imperialism of the West, fearing Turkey and its sister Islamic republics achieving political, military and economic power and strength in the Middle East, are now sending the Crusaders' commandant, John Paul, anointed as religious leader, to Turkey. If this visit is not cancelled I will kill the commandant Pope.

According to several analysts of the case there are serious doubts that the failed murderer wrote this letter. On the other hand, the tone and manner were similar to that of the Iranian leadership, who would refer to John Paul II as 'Pope Commandant' or 'The Crusades Commandant'. Following this theory, Ali Agca would have been trained in the Iranian terrorist camps. There they gave him his mission and told him that the Pope had come to power on the same day as the Shah of Persia had been dethroned in the Iranian Islamic Revolution. The parallel was as clear as it was simple: the end of Pope Wojtyla would coincide with the Islamic Revolution achieving its ends.

All this information was gathered by Mossad, the Israeli intelligence service. Apparently, this agency had been trying to get achieve a rapprochment with the Vatican for some years and providing the secret information about an affair that worried the Pope so much was a good way to do so. Nevertheless, that is also the reason why some doubts are raised. With this information to hand, John Paul II gave his support to Israel in its struggles with the Arab world. This stance greatly influenced public opinion. To what extent was the information provided by Mossad true? Was it just a bluff to get the support of the Pope? This remains a mystery today, and one to which is is very difficult to obtain a clear answer.

As can be seen, the schemes and conspiracies of the Vatican are not all in the past. One must ask oneself: could there be someone already planning the death of the pope? Who would benefit most from his disappearance – secret societies inspired by the esoteric Illuminati or specific groups within the Church?

9. The Complex World of the Vatican

The Vatican, the main setting for Dan Brown's novel, is a unique city-state. It scarcely covers half a square kilometre. It is only a tiny corner on the map of Rome, but it has incredible power spanning the entire globe. Not for nothing does its Supreme Pontiff have formal spiritual authority over more than eight hundred million people.

Nevertheless, the Holy See, which governs with absolute power, has no natural resources or factories; it does not possess armies, land that produces fruit, pasture, rivers, valleys or ports... The Vatican is just a maze of palaces and gardens with an old railway station and a asic heliport. Its population barely reaches 1,000 most of them Italians and Swiss with a few people of other nationalities.

The head of state must be male and holds the post for life. The chosen one does not need to comply with the norms imposed in other states: to be born or be a national of the country.

In the Vatican, evidently, there are no political parties, no opposition leaders or electoral campaigns, but there is a large number of lobbies that fight for power behind the throne. This is why it is easy to understand why the Vatican has been, and always will be, an extraordinary centre of attention for politicians, the religious and intellectuals; a place where faith and secrecy operate side by side.

It all started centuries ago on an arid and inhospitable piece of land, the *Ager Vaticanus* (stony place of the Vatican), on the right bank of the Tiber (or Tevere) between the Monte Mario and Janiculum. It was no-man's-land; it did not belong to Rome and was not within its boundaries. An Etruscan community had previously inhabited it; they came from an old village called Vaticum.

The Romans had defeated the Etruscans in the Battle of Veyes (396 BC) so the Ager Vaticanus was already a part of Rome when Saint Peter was crucified there upside down. Later, to commemorate the Pope's martyrdom they built the old Basilica of Saint Peter at the bottom of the Vatican Hill, and a bridge, the Pons Aelius, connecting the Vatican to Rome. There is archaeological evidence today that points to the tomb of the Apostle being under the main altar of the Basilica. In fact, there is a document dated from AD 160 that makes reference to this altar stating, 'Peter is here'.

Pope Pius XII gave an order, in 1939, to dig what would be the tomb of Pius XI. When they started digging they found a mosaic. In front of them lay the Necropolis, with magnificent mausolea of important Roman families, but there was also a small tomb, which was open and empty. The small space was protected by walls to preserve the inside from rain, and it was full of hundreds of Roman and medieval coins from different parts of Europe, an indication that the person buried there had been venerated throughout the continent. There were other details to indicate this was the apostle's tomb. Despite all this proof, Pius XII did not confirm it until several years later when, during his 1950 Christmas address, he said, 'We have found Saint Peter's tomb'.

A JEWEL IN HALF A SQUARE KILOMETRE

In 1929 the Lateran Treaty confirmed the terrestrial power of the Popes with the creation of the independent state of the Vatican. On this Pius XI declared: 'This territory is small but we can say it is the largest in the world, because it has a colonnade by Bernini, a dome made by Michelangelo and immense scientific volumes in its libraries, beautiful gardens and galleries, not to mention the prince of apostles' tomb'. He was not far wrong. The Vatican is a real but concentrated treasure on a tiny parcel of land.

It is important to stress that most of those riches are kept in the Vatican Museum, which boasts an impressive collection of the most significant geniuses in the history of art: Michelangelo, Leonardo da Vinci, Raphael, Murillo, Ribera, Giulio Romano, Titian, Paolo Veronese, Caravaggio, Moretto… It is hardly surprising that this art gallery is considered one of the most impressive in the world and that the Vatican complex officially forms part of the Roman World Heritage Site. It is said that it takes ten minutes to walk across the city but a whole life to contemplate its artistic wealth.

WHAT IS HIDDEN IN THE SECRET ARCHIVES?

The Central Archives of the Vatican, better known using the suggestive name of the Secret Archives, are right next to the Vatican's Library. The reality is, and to cut short any fantasies, that this is where all documents related to minutes, pastoral activities and the running of Vatican are stored. It is true that it has always been surrounded by a halo of mystery that provoked all kinds of extreme speculation, most of it unfounded. Perhaps its name is to blame, but it must be understood that in this case the word 'secret' means 'private', the same word used for the archives in kingdoms and dynasties who kept hidden the darkest or most glorious pages of their entire history.

Inside the Vatican Library, a room brimming with mystery and legend

The Secret Archives of the Vatican were built in the 17th century under Paul V's orders. The Pontiff had decided to gather all documents written by the Church in its history. However, in reality most of the documents found date from the fourth century onwards, exactly the era of the first archive building; it was built in Saint John Lateran, where it stayed until the end of the 12th century. The Archive of Ancient Manuscripts was later created in the Castel Sant'Angelo. In time, internal battles, pillage and continuous transfers led to the loss of many valuable documents.

The creation of the Secret Archives rescued the documents they possessed and enabled them to keep new ones safe. In 1881, Leo XIII granted access to any researchers who wanted to explore its treasures. Today, all kinds of documents can be found, some of them truly peculiar, like the letters Lucrezia Borgia wrote to her father, Pope Alexander VI; several notes from Martin Luther and Rossini; and even love letters from Henry VIII to Ann Boleyn. All of this is very interesting but these documents cannot genuinely be qualified as secret. There are no documents on the secret of the Holy Grail, the Illuminati conspiracies or on the relationship between the Church and Freemasonry. Unless there is a secret door behind the shelves of the library that lead to another archive, the really secret one.

THE SECRETS OF THE VATICAN CURIA

Standing out amid the Vatican's turbulent history is the Roman Curia, a group of people in high-ranked positions and clerical civil servants working and living inside the Holy See. Their function is to assist the Pope who needs back-up from political or theological departments, and from administration and legal offices to fulfill his mission as the supreme pastor of the Church.

The Secretary of State's office is the part of the Roman Curia that mostly closely to the Pope. Its history starts in 1487 when the Apostolic Office, made up of twenty-four secretariats, was instituted, One of the secretaries, the *Saecretarius Domusticus*, also known simply as the Pope's secretary, holds the position of honour among them, and is in charge of the most personal matters. Centuries later, Pius VII created the Holy Congregation for Extraordinary Ecclesiastical Affairs. A century later it was divided into three departments: extraordinary affairs, ordinary affairs and pontifical briefs. In 1967, Paul VI scrapped the third department and the Holy Congregation became the Council for the Public Affairs of the Church.

In 1988 John Paul II made another reform dividing the Secretary of State's office into two sections: general affairs and foreign affairs. The former section, managed by an archbishop with the help of a prelate, is in charge of the Pope's daily activities, it arranges audiences, drafts his documents, processes nominations and, in addition to many other tasks, has custody of the Pope's stamped lead seal and the fisherman's ring. The second section arranges the state's affairs, deals with diplomatic business, represents the Vatican internationally and announces the nominations of bishops in other countries. This section is directed by an archbishop who is the 'secretary for foreign affairs' and is assisted by another prelate as under secretary. The Secretariat of State, home of these two sections, is chaired

---

The Devil's advocate

There is a tale that says that the Devil himself enjoyed insidiously questioning aspiring saints on their claimed miracles, so he asked the Pope to set him up with an advocate at the Vatican to take over his role. The Pontiff thought this a justified request and named a prelate to do the job. The post has the official title of Faith Promoter, but popular tradition has always called it the 'Devil's advocate'.

The canonization of a person considered sufficiently exceptional can only occur a certain time after the person's death, and generally after a petition from communities or institutions able to give testimony of his or her pious life and goodness, as well as the miracles he or she has performed. The meeting at which it is decided whether or not to approve the canonization is like a form of judicial trial with a sole judge whose verdict is final – the Pope. But to make his decision he must listen to the advocate of the 'defendant', who will detail the virtues and merits of his 'client' to prove his sanctity, and to the 'prosecutor' who will try to refute with objections. The former is the 'Postulator' or 'God's advocate'. The latter is our well-known 'Devil's advocate'.

---

by a cardinal with the title 'Secretary of State' and he is the Pope's main assistant in governing the Church. He is responsible for any political activity and diplomatic affairs in the Vatican.

There is another very influential body – the 'Bishops' Synod', a permanent institution created by Paul VI in 1965, with the aim of trying to keep the spiritual flame lit by the experience gained from Vatican II alive. It is essentially an assembly of bishops and the Pope, formed to exchange information and experiences, and to find solutions to pastoral issues.

THE COMPLICATED PROCESS OF ELECTING A POPE

In the plot of *Angels and Demons*, the Pope has died and the conclave has been called to meet. The Pauline Chapel, like the Sistine adorned with Michelangelo frescoes, is where the cardinals meet for Mass before electing a new Pope. There, those called to fulfil such a mission must listen to a serious sermon to remind them of their supreme obligation to provide the Church with the son most capable of providing direction and guidance.

In reality, the Conclave is not solely the election of a pope, it is much more. It is a struggle for supreme power in the Church, motivated by doctrinal and ideological differences; candidates' supporters will need to win other members' votes and establish alliances to make sure that their candidate will be the one finally elected. However, it is a common saying that 'he who goes into the Conclave as Pope, will leave as a cardinal'. Very often none of the factions wins the majority needed, which means there has to be an agreement to elect a third man as happened with the election of Celestine V and John Paul I.

Following the death of a Pontiff there is a provisional period which is known as the *Sede Vacante* (the empty throne). During this time the Roman Curia is ruled by the principle of *'Nihil Innovatur'* – 'no change'. Although the Church's government is in the hands of the College of Cardinals, they may only make routine and simple decisions. After 15 days from the death of the Pope, the cardinals must form the Conclave to choose Christ's new Vicar and during this period the Camerlengo possesses some power.

In Dan Brown's novel the Camerlengo has considerable power although in reality he is little more than a butler, and as the late Pope's civil servant must see to the protocol for the election of the new Pontiff. He invites all the cardinals from around the world, confirms their attendance, greets them at the Holy See and ensures readiness on the day the Conclave meets. The word *'camerlengo'* comes from the Latin *'camerarius'* (from the chamber), referring to the place where the treasure was kept. In the monastic world, the camerlengo was the monk in charge of administrating the parish's goods, a kind of a treasurer. This is how we arrive at the Holy See's camerlengo, who initially administered the possessions and the income of the Vatican but whose powers were restricted from the beginning of the 19th century by Pope Pius VII. Today, the camerlengo is in charge of verifying the Pope's death and of assisting the Great Elector during the Conclave's proceedings.

The role of camerlengo is not easy but it is not as difficult as the role of Great Elector. Inside the secretive Conclave the Great Elector, also known as the Master of Ceremonies, organizes the voting procedures and ensures step-by-step adherence to protocol.

A delicate gesture by Pope Jean Paul II

It is said that, newly nominated as the next Pope, John Paul II accepted the Conclave cardinals' congratulations but did not sit on the throne as tradition dictates. Instead he remained standing, waiting for the cardinals to parade in front of him. When the Master of Ceremonies invited him to take a seat he replied: 'no, thank you, I will stand up to welcome my brothers'.

The word 'conclave' comes from the Latin *cum clavis*, meaning 'locked with a key'. This is because the election of the new Pope occurs behind locked doors to avoid the participants contacting the outer world. The select group of cardinals required to undertake such a high mission is in its majority composed of pastors from dioceses, some of which are far flung. Tradition states that the electing members must be prelates of Rome so, during the process, they are granted 'honorary titles' from one of Rome's churches.

Cardinals have not always enjoyed such an important role in the election of a Pope. In reality neither Holy Scripture or tradition dictate how a Supreme Pontiff should be elected. In fact, it is supposed that the first Popes just pointed out their own successors. It would later be Rome's Bishop who would fill the post. In 1059, Pope Nicholas II decreed that a group of cardinals would elect his successor and those who came after. In 1179, the Lateran Council established that two-thirds of the votes must be gained to anoint a candidate – a rule that still applies.

In February 1996, John Paul II, promulgated the document 'On the Vacancy in the Apostolic See and the Election of the Roman Pontiff', in which he provided clear instructions on how the election of his successor should be conducted.

It is evident that most of the indications and notes that the Pontiff gave were based on strict traditional rules. On the day of his death there would be no great changes; the process was to be practically identical to those of the past, except for a few naunces.

The Camerlengo, Cardinal Eduardo Martinez Somalo, was instructed to call John Paul by his name three times, and on receiving no reply, declare, 'The Pope is dead.' His next task would be to destroy the personal seal and the famous Fisherman's Ring immediately to avoid forgery. Only then could he announce the death of the Supreme Pontiff to the Dean of the College of Cardinals.

After this the Camerlengo was to seal the Pope's chambers and organize the Conclave to begin between fifteen and twenty days after the death of the Pope. The Conclave was to meet in absolute secrecy and, following his Holiness's instructions, in an atmosphere of quietness and prayer.

The cardinals were directed to meet on the day of the election in the beautiful setting of the Basilica of Saint Peter to celebrate a votive mass called 'Pro Eligendo Papa' in order to ease the tense atmosphere of the pre-election meetings and any nervousness about voting, especially if who would be elected was not obvious. Later they had to go in solemn procession to the Sistine Chapel, bearing in mind that when they emerged, the would be subjects of one of their number, who they would have designated Supreme Pontiff.

The cardinals were directed to elect the new Pope behind locked doors in the Sistine Chapel, swearing to honour 'absolute and perpetual' silence. Ecclesiastic penalties for breaching the oaths could be as severe as excommunication. The apostolic document, written and signed by John Paul II, even stated how the piece of paper, on which the cardinals wrote their chosen name, should be folded and the name written.

If the votes did not achieve a the majority needed, the electors had to spend as many nights as needed inside the Vatican, at the Domus

Inside the Sistine Chapel, where behind locked doors the cardinals choose the new Pope

Sanctae Marthae, a residence opened in 1996 as lodgings for Curia staff.
John Paul II tried to ensure that the Conclave would not be a long one by
ruling out the possibility of election by acclamation and insisting that the
vote should take place in absolute secrecy to eliminate the possibility of
discussion amongst the cardinals.

Following tradition, after each voting session, the electors had to
inform the faithful gathered outside of the results, using the system that
been used for centuries: a column of smoke. If a winner has not yet been
consecrated, dry straw is burned to give black smoke. But if a new Pope has
been chosen, wet straw is burned to give the famous 'fumata Bianca' that
the masses celebrate with devout enthusiasm.

Finally, once a consensus was reached and been made public, all
the ballots were to be burned. The Dean of the College of Cardinals was to
address the new Pope to ask him if he accepted his election. If he did, he
was then to tell the Conclave by what Papal name he would like to be
known to history. After this ritual the cardinals were to pay homage, then
the senior cardinal deacon could announce Urbi et orbi – the good news –
from the balcony of the basilica, in the traditional way.

Mass celebrated by his Holiness John Paul II in the main altar of Saint Peter's Basilica

APPENDICES

APPENDIX 1
The Hash-Ashin: Terrifying and Deadly

In the book *Angels and Demons* a man is given the task of kidnapping and murdering of four Papal candidates. He executes them in specific places, following a supposed Illuminati ritual. But the most important thing is that in the first few pages he is said to belong to a dangerous old sect:

His ancestors created a small but deadly army... They became famous, not only for their brutal massacres, but for committing their assassinations in a drug-induced state... These deadly men were known by one word 'hash-ashin', literally 'hashish followers'...

The hash-ashin sect has always maintained a worryingly confrontational relationship with the Vatican. They are of Islamic origin and never forgave the Knights Templar for copying their symbols and organization. Many historians believe that they died out centuries ago, but recent investigations show that the society still functions. Furthermore, there are those who believe that some Islamic terrorist groups belong to them.

To understand this secret society we need to submerge ourselves into their history. Firstly, their name is sinister enough. However, more thorough research has revealed that it stems from their liking for hashish, not their criminal practices. They were called 'hashishis' – hashish eaters. Whenever we try to penetrate secret societies many questions are raised, but hardly any answers found. With reference to the Hash-ashin sect, researchers seem to agree that its activities started in the 11th century. Its founder was Hassan-Ben-Sabbah, a Persian born in Khorossan (now in Iran). This Islamic warrior took possession of the Alamut Fortress, in North Persia, and proclaimed himself to be the reincarnation of the last imam. Many decided to follow his relaxed cult: they smoked Indian hemp during their continuous

Hassan Ben-Sabbah, according to an old print, leader of the Assassins sect

ceremonies. He lived until he was ninety, very unusual for the time, because of a good lifestyle. When Hassan died in 1124, he had a legion of followers ready to fight against the Christians. Their fierce character gained them victory in nearly all battles, and they even forced the Knights Templar, their biggest enemies, to pay them tribute. At that time, the Knights Templar copied the structure and organization of the Hash-ashin.

Because of their drugs consumption and their continuous orgies, many researchers believe that the Assassins were simply a sect of opportunistic warriors but there was a profound spirituality behind their actions. For example, it has been said that the first fortress they built was an exact replica of Mohamed's paradise, with all the women and drugs promised by the prophet to his followers.

Although they were essentially an Islamic sect, the Assassins also absorbed aspects of other beliefs. In fact, nearly all researchers believe their doctrine is based on Gnosis, Kabbala and alchemy. These are religious strands that have always been intimately linked with esotericism, and which aspire to a very high level of knowledge achievable by only a few. Their organization was hierarchical basically because they did not differentiate between Good and Bad; their only duty was to obey the imam. To them, Good and Bad were parts of the same entity, therefore it was the same to follow one as the other.

A PARADISE OF LUXURY AND KNOWLEDGE

The headquarters of the Hash-hasins was the Fortress of Alamut, which was designed as a copy of Paradise. There, those assassins who had carried out important missions (a commissioned murder, for example) would be rewarded by enjoying a few weeks' holiday. But this was not simply a place for pleasure, it also housed an Astronomical observatory and one of the largest Science and Philosophy libraries in the Ancient World, whose secrets were carefully guarded. If a member revealed those secrets he would be executed by his colleagues according to gruesome rituals.

Nevertheless, some members must have sold out to the Christians or squealed under torture, because both Knights Templar and Freemasons copied the precious architectural secrets, which showed in their stone places of worship. A different group was responsible for each part of the building process to ensure no one would have an overall idea of how it could have been built. The orientation of these buildings reveals that they took advantage of the lines of force of the planet, placing them in particularly energetic locations. They engraved esoteric symbols in their temples, as the Freemasons were later to do.

The Hash-ashin sructure, which was more or less plagiarized by the Knights Templar, gave the apprentices the rank of 'lassik', a kind of servant who attended all the other members of the group. If a lassik did his job well he would then be promoted to 'fidavi', a squire under the orders of one or more warriors. These were the 'refic', knights who went to war and carried out assassinations on the instructions of the head of the society. If they accomplished these deeds and learned the secrets of the sect, they would then become 'Dais', the advisors of the 'Old Man of the Mountain', which was the name given to the imam. This was the highest rank and his orders had to be obeyed by all his followers. It was, therefore, a strictly pyramidal society, one very easy to join but very difficult to climb. Many believe that when they fled from Genghis Khan's persecution, they dispersed and became killers for hire.

The ruins of the Fortress of Alamut (Syria today), refuge to members of the Assassins sect

APPENDIX 2
Can the Vatican be Blown up by an Antimatter Bomb?

Upon reading *Angels and Demons*, a question arises: is it possible to use antimatter technolocy to blow up a whole city? To answer this question main reference points that spring up from the text will be analysed in an attempt to clear up the obscure boundary between fact and fiction.

CERN, A PIONEER CENTRE

The European Council for Nuclear Research, or CERN in its French acronym, is the scientific body that has created the product capable of blowing up the Vatican in Dan Brown's novel. What is CERN really? Where are they based? To what extent has Brown taken literary licence too far?

CERN is one of the most advanced research centres in the world. It has contributed to the advancement of science in a fantastic way and practically all experts in the matter believe that it will keep its position at

Aerial view of CERN's compound in Meyrin, on the French–Swiss border

the forefront in the future. Nuclear physics, sadly, has always been associated with lethal armaments and weapons of destruction, since that fatal August when Hiroshima and Nagasaki suffered the first attack of the kind. Nevertheless, the possibilities of nuclear physics are not limited to the production of only this kind of bomb. There are many kinds of applications, from the familiar nuclear energy to other innumerable possibilities.

CERN was founded in 1954 by twelve European countries. Today it has twenty member states, 500 associated universities from 80 nations and 6,500 scientists, some of whom are Nobel prize-winners. Its headquarters are in Meyrin, on the Franco–Swiss border. Among the many achievements and awards received by the body for its research, the best-known is, without a doubt, 'www', the World Wide Web, the internet system produced in this laboratory and patented in 1990.

THE PARTICLES ACCELERATOR

Certainly the most brilliant CERN experiments are those based on the particle accelerator and all its current and future scientific possibilities. But starting from the beginning: what is a particle accelerator? It is a basic instrument in high energy physics. It is several kilometres long and building and maintaining it cost a fortune, but it has great benefits and results.

The function of the accelerator is, as its name clearly states, to accelerate particles (protons, neutrons, electrons and atomic nuclei or ions) close to light speed. The object of accelerating them is to transmit large amounts of energy to the particles so that they collide into each other or against a fixed target. When the particles collide, phenomena in the atomic structure that would otherwise be invisible can be detected. To gain a more approximate idea, the accelerators are basically very long tubes with electromagnets placed at intervals to ensure that the particles do not disperse and they continue on the correct path. There are two types of accelerator: linear and circular. Because of their large volume both are built underground. The most modern, and the most popular, are the synchrotrons, which can reach unbelievable speed.s During the experiments, the accelerators can consume up to 60 MWh of electricity.

Today Spain, together with several other European countries, is building a new more powerful accelerator in the Technological Park of Valles, Catalonia. The cost of the project has been estimated at 120 million euros, and it should be finished by 2008.

NUCLEAR FISSION

Of all applications a particle accelerator possesses, the best known is nuclear fission. We should take into account that the first particle accelerator, built in 1930, led to the discovery of the neutron and the positron.

That discovery was fundamental to the development of nuclear physics. Until that time, it was impossible to split protons (positive electrical charge) or electrons (negative electrical charge), because when there was an attempt to bombard them, they would either repel or attract each other. This is why both particles seemed indivisible. But, when the neutron, which has no positive or negative electrical charge, was discovered, scientists realized they could use it to bombard other particles and create new energies.

So, nuclear fission consists of bombarding a heavy atomic nucleus with neutrons. It will then split into two nuclei, one with half the mass of the other. This process releases a great deal of energy and two or three neutrons. These cause more collisions when they bump into the new nuclei. A kind of chain reaction is thus achieved. Every collision produces energy higher than the one before in thousandths of a second. This runaway fission is the principle on which the nuclear bomb works but if the rate of fission reactions is controlled, only one of the freed neutrons produces secondary fission. Nuclear fission energy is based upon this principle.

ANTIMATTER

When the first particle accelerator was unveiled, the scientists realized that the atom and the nucleus would have no more secrets from that moment on. A particle accelerator allows practically anything to be done with them. For example, it can divide them, join them, change them... but within the frame of all these investigations, there is one aspect in particular that draws researchers' attention and which is subject to different exotic theories: antimatter.

Before we discuss this theory, we must understand its basic principle by looking at antiparticles. Protons and electrons have a different electrical charge (positive and negative) and also different weight. What would happen if a proton (positive electrical charge) with the same mas as an electron was created? We would have an anti-electron. But the key question here is, what would happen when both crashed into each other? Total destruction. The clash would provoke a huge energy, far superior to any known now.

Photograph of CERN's tunnel

With the opening of CERN in 1978, experiments of this kind were carried out. In 1981, the first controlled collission between matter and antimatter was carried out. The results showed that the amount of energy released was huge, a thousand times bigger than nuclear energy released until then. It was time to go from antiparticles to anti-atoms, which are extremely difficult to create. To produce them required a combination of various antiparticles, but attempts were unsuccessful. The basic problem was the high speed at which the antimatter particles were produced, and the rapid, destructive collisions. It was vital to find a way to slow them down and qualize their speed in order to combine them and create the antiatom. The work of Stan Brodsky, Ivan Schmidt and Charles Munger found a way of combining antielectrons and antiprotons, and CERN embarked upon a project with the objective of creating an antiatom.

On 4 January 1996, the scientists at CERN announced the successful production of nine hydrogen antiatoms. Using hydrogen was not a arbitrary choice: apart from being the most basic element, it is the most abundant in the whole of the Universe. The basic problem was that if the antimatter touched any matter it would destroy it. How could it be retained? The scientists created a complicated electromagnetic system to hold it suspended. This achievement opens the door to the study of antimatter, a unique opportunity to test the laws of Physics.

In fact, the electromagnetic system is the one depicted in *Angels and Demons*. In this case the novel plays with fiction, although it is based in fact.

SCIENCE AND FICTION

Hopefully in the next few years important conclusions will be reached about the behaviour of antimatter, which will certainly permit the explanation of cosmic phenomena that have been a mystery until today; for example, how is antimatter produced in the Universe? Antimatter could provide extremely cheap and unlimited energy, which would give a definite boost to aerospace: great speeds could be reached and the secrets of the Universe uncovered. But scientists must also acknowledge its highly negative aspect: that if applied incorrectly such a powerful source of energy could also be used in a truly catastrophic way.

APPENDIX 3
Science, Technology and Religion

The relationship between science and religion has always been controversial. All religions were created with the aim of answering the questions that humans could not. With the advance of science, that function is slowly being eroded. Every day there are more and more answers from the scientific field that do not require a religious explanation. Nevertheless, there is still a subject that the Catholic Church will not relinquish in any way: the existence of God. This is the dogma on which the whole faith is founded, and no Catholic is included recognize any kind of investigation or research in which the existence of God is questioned.

However, there have been researchers who have put together theories about this matter. These are the most relevant.

THE PROBLEM OF STUDYING GOD

One of the main problems that scientist encounter is that they do their research based on proof, behaviour or experiment, and in the case of an entity like God, this is to all intents and purposes impossible. What initial evidence could be used as a basis for the research? Only faith, which apart from always being subjective, is not a very scientific argument. This is why there is no possibility of even starting serious research. The Church puts

Moses, guide for the people of Israel passing through the Red Sea and later, on their travels through the desert

forward as proof the existence of the Universe. And this continues to be one of the great existentialist questions of science: how it all began.

Evolution can explain the presence of man on Earth, the existence of water justifies life, the Big Bang and the the creation of our planet. But there is always a last aspect that science cannot access. This explains how all these discoveries cannot come into conflict with the concept of God. Albert Einstein once said that the more he knew about science the more he was convinced of the existence of God.

Many scientists have refuted many of the Church's beliefs but have continued believing in the Supreme Being. Bear in mind that the Church is still reticent about the theory of evolution, which is totally accepted by the scientific community. Most scientists are very cautious about this question: because the existence of God cannot be confirmed or denied, it is best not to express any opinion on such a delicate matter.

ASPECTS QUESTIONED BY SCIENCE

Because of a lack of proof, in the past scientists have not dared to give their opinion on the existence of God, but they have contradicted the Church in other matters. Here is a look at some of them:

• **The origin of the world** is one of the main topics. There are more theories every day looking to explain how the Universe and the Earth were formed, and they have virtually nothing to do with the stories told in Genesis. The Big Bang is the current scientific model upon which they base their theories.

• **The presence of man on Earth** is another point of conflict. Science has proved that it is impossible for the whole of the human race to originate from one couple as explained in the Bible.

• **Some aspects of the Holy Scriptures** have been demythologized by diverse investigations that have tried to give rational to things that were presented as supernatural. Manna for example, could be the product of an atmospheric phenomenon that occurs in the desert. The parting of the Red Sea could have a physical explanation to it. Even Lazarus' resurrection could possibly have been caused by an illness.

In this way, science has been able to give an explanation to nearly all the actions attributed to God, but it still has no arguments to deny or confirm his existence.

A TEST-TUBE GOD

One of the subjects of major debate is the possibility of a test-tube God. The argument develops as follows: if man the ability of cloning another human being, who is to say that in a century or millennium he could not do the same thing with the Universe? This theory has made some people accept that God may have created the Universe, but that if so, he must be superior being cloned by an advanced civilization and this would have very little to do with the mystical conception of his existence.

On the other hand, some believe that genetic manipulation could lead to the ability to create a God. These theories are somehow very far from reality but they have increasingly more followers. God is human perfection; we are only a bad copy of him. Therefore, if it is possible to create such a perfect human, are we so far from creating a God?

This ignites theological debates that worry both ecclesiastics and atheists. In fact, in Brown's book, we can clearly see that the plot also has vengeance against the Church, but in the name of science. The Illuminati are no more than defendants of those other scientists (Galileo was one of them), who centuries ago dared believe another theory about the conception of the world and of God. As the novel develops we see that, with the excuse of vengeance for the centuries of repression science has suffered, at attempt is made to eliminate God's representative on Earth using science, at least from the point of view of the Catholic cult. Perhaps the best way to understand the conflict between God and science is to use, by way of a conclusion, quotes from some of the world's greatest scientists:

'Every serious scientist must possess a type of religious feeling, because he cannot imagine that the extremely minute connections that he is observing, are being observed for the first time, by him. In the Universe, which it is impossible to grasp, a manifestation of a superior and infinite Intelligence is being revealed.'

ALBERT EINSTEIN

'I have never denied the existence of God. I believe that the Theory of Evolution is absolutely compatible with the belief in God. The fact that it is impossible to prove or grasp that the amazing and above every measure beautiful universe as well as mankind came into being by coincidence seem to be the main evidence for the existence of God.'

CHARLES DARWIN

'Who living in intimate contact with the most consummate of orders and the divine knowledge will not feel stimulated by the most sublime aspirations? Who would not adore the architect of all these things?'

NICOLAS COPERNICUS

'All my respects and maximum admiration goes to all engineers, especially to the greatest of all, God.'

THOMAS A. EDISON

APPENDIX 4
The Secret Route of *Angels and Demons*

Within the pages of *Angels and Demons* we discover a great number of places where the author gives his own interpretation of locations linking them to the Illuminati plot.

To guide the eager reader this brief appendix will be dedicated to the real history of the novel's 'setting' at the time when our characters are already in Rome.

1. THE FABULOUS BASILICA OF SAINT PETER

The most beautiful site in theVatican City is the Basilica of Saint Peter. As mentioned in the introduction, the tomb of the Apostle, located under the high altar, is the centre of its structure. In front of it, and next to the four bases of the enormous cupola of the Basilica, we can see very large statues representing Saint Longinus, Saint Veronica, Saint Andrew and Saint Helena.

It is precisely above the statue of Saint Helena that, on very rare occasions, beautiful relics, like a piece of what is supposed to be part of Jesus' cross, are shown to the public. Above the four enormous

Saint Peter's Basilica, one of the artistic wonders of the West and the largest building in the Christian world

representations of these saints are very elaborate mosaics depicting the four Evangelists. Above this huge mosaic and surrounding the entire base of the cupola, a Latin inscription can be read: 'You are Peter, and on this rock I will build my Church, and I will give you the keys of heaven.'

On the right hand side of Saint Peter's Basilica's main nave, near the entrance, one can see Michelangelo's famous *Pieta*. Amid this impressive architecture are the tombs of Saint Gregory, Leo II, Leo III, LEO IV, John XXIII, and Paul IV, amongst others.

2. THE SISTINE CHAPEL: A HOMAGE TO ART

The eyes of more than ten million visitors annually received by the Vatican usually search eagerly for one of its greatest treasures: the Sistine Chapel. The Holy See has many chapels but this, commissioned by Pope Sixtus VI, is doubtless the most famous of all. The architect was Giovanni de Dolci, who dedicated himself entirely from 1473 to 1481, to what would become his greatest work.

But if its architectural structure is impressive, the quality and quantity of its frescoes is even more so. All walls are covered with the work of the most significant artists of the time. From Perugino to Botticelli, from Salviati to Matteo da Lecce. But, without doubt, Michelangelo occupies the highest rank with his *Creation*, the extraordinary fresco covering the entire Chapel ceiling.

Frescoes at the Sistine Chapel. Commissioned by Pope Julius II of Michelangelo, they took four years of intensive work to complete

As well as all the compliments that the Sistine Chapel received there was also criticism, for example, from the Master of Ceremonies Biagio da Cesena, who said that 'It was a very indecent thing for such an honourable place to have so many naked paintings that so indecently show their shameful parts.' He also said that this was not work for the Pope's chapel but was more appropriate for thermal baths or taverns.

In 1564 these polemic words led the Council of Trent's Congregation to cover some of the figures. In adding drapes, which they called 'breeches', was Daniele de Volterra who was subsequently known as the 'braghettone' (the breeches-dresser).

3. AGRIPPA'S PANTHEON

This is a Roman temple dedicated to the seven planetary gods. It has been called the cathedral of the pagan world although the truth is that two deities, Venus and Mars, were the main divinities of this place.

The Pantheon is named after Agrippa because it was the consul Agrippa, Augustus' son-in-law, who gave the order for its construction in 27 BC. The temple suffered many fires and it was not until AD 126 that it was reconstructed, supposedly by Apollodoro of Damascus.

Piazza del Pantheon, oil painting by Vincenzo Giovannini. The Pantheon is a magnificent temple dedicated to all gods, built by Hadrian in the second century AD in the centre of Ancient Rome

The Pantheon of Agrippa claims to be a synthesis of Roman religious feelings. In fact, its object was to group all the gods' dwellings into one place, therefore it represents a union of heaven and earth, in a circular base closed up by a large cupola.

On the highest walls there recesses were made to house the figures representing the different Roman gods. Michelangelo said that this building's design was angelic and not human.

4. THE DEMON'S HOLE

The Demon's Hole or Oculus is mentioned in the book *Angels and Demons*, although its protagonists later seek the 'Buco Diavolo'. The demon's hole mentioned is really the cupola of Agrippa's Pantheon. The building is 43.20 metres both in interior height and in diameter. The effect of such a cupola in a circular building suggests the representation of a great celestial globe resting on the ground. The Pantheon's builders, when installing such a spectacular cupola, wanted to achieve a sense of closeness to the celestial realm where their gods lived.

Inside the Pantheon, oil painting by G. P. Pannini. The Demon's Hole is the opening at the top of Agrippa's Pantheon

5. RAPHAEL'S TOMB

This is located inside Agrippa's Pantheon, In the Renaissance the Church ordered a list of changes to be made inside the Pantheon. The chapels were filled with works of art and were home to the tombs of historical, illustrious characters, such as Raphael de Urbino, which is in one of the old chapels where the Roman deities were once found.

The master painter and architect was born in Urbino on 6 April 1483 and died in 1520. His mother had him baptized with the name of the archangel representing spring time and beauty.

Raphael grew up in a refined and calm environment – Urbino was a centre of culture at the time. His father encouraged him to study painting and this ignited in him the desire to master drawing, particularly perspective.

In 1494, Raphael was left as an orphan under the tutelage of his paternal brother. They did not enjoy a good relationship as the tutor did not appreciate of the boy's artistic talent. But Raphael's luck changed when a year later a young artist, Timoteo Viti, came onto the scene in Urbino and took Raphael as his apprentice and servant. Some time later the young artist moved into the hands of another painter, one of the most renowned in Florence, Pietro Vanucci. Raphael was only 17 when he went on to a more complex painting technique with Perugino; he worked with him in Florence for several years and by the time he became independent he was a great master with the brush. In fact, Raphael excelled on his own from the beginning of the 16th century.

Raphael started to come to the attention of major patrons and to receive requests from the most significant of them, who considered him a genius. In 1504 Pope Julius II, aware of his artistic capabilities, asked him to decorate his living quarters at the Vatican. Today, Julius II rooms are known as the Raphael Stanze. Inside them, Raphael painted one of the most famous fresco cycles known in history. In between 1509 and 1511 he decorated the Stanza della Signatura, where he painted several allegorical scenes representing Theology, Philosophy, Poetry and Justice on the four medallions of the vault.

Tomb of Raphael of Urbino, where the artist's remains lie

The Chigi Chapel, by Raphael with sculptures by Bernini and Lorenzetto

In 1514 he was named Great Master of the Basilica of Saint Peter, and a year later he was made responsible for all archaeological excavations carried out in Rome and its surroundings. Raphael also planned the architecte and the decoration for the Chigi Chapel in the Church of Santa Maria del Popolo.

The truth is that there are no references of links to the secret societies of the time, but he did keep good relations, although discreetly, with alchemists and the esoteric, let us not forget the significance of his link to the Papacy through all those commissions.

6. THE CHIGI CHAPEL

This chapel was a present to Agostino Chigi by Pope Julius II, as well as a chapel in Santa Maria della Pace.

The Chigi Chapel, which has a very curious hexagonal shape and was designed by Raphael, is inside the Santa Maria del Popolo. It is common knowledge that by then Raphael had become so famous he no longer went to the sites but that his most talented assistants were the ones who did the work.

7. SANTA MARIA DEL POPOLO

This temple is located in the Piazza del Popolo. It is a church started in 1099 next to the old Roman city walls. Due to some existing structural problems, Pope Sixtus V ordered its reconstruction in 1477. But the basilica still had some architectural faults so Bernini was commissioned to do a further reconstruction in the 17th century.

According to stories of the time, before the basilica was built the area was haunted by Nero's ghost who infested the place with evil spirits that would come out from the pyramidal mausoleum to molest the Christians. After a public petition, the Pope Paschal II performed an exorcism on the place cutting down a walnut tree that had grown over an old tomb that was then demolished and thrown into the river Tiber. The church was built over the site of the mausoleum.

8. PIAZZA DEL POPOLO

This is a open area, which is dominated by obelisk in the middle and one of the first Renaissance churches built in Rome, Santa Maria del Popolo. The history of the square is quite peculiar.

According to records, the original square existed in Roman times, more specifically in the 1st century AD. Agrippina, the wife of the Emperor Claudius, decided to have her tomb there and ordered it to be built in the shape of a pyramid. The current square has little to do with the original. It was restructured during the first years of the 19th century during the Napoleonic occupation (1808–1814); the oval was extended and four lion fountains were built around the obelisk.

9. THE OBELISK IN THE PIAZZA DEL POPOLO

This is by far the tallest obelisk in Rome and thought to be around 3,000 years old. It was erected in Rome on the orders of Emperor Augustus after it was brought here from Luxor in Egypt, where Rameses II had it constructed.

Wanting to impress visitors Augustus decided the best place for the obelisk would be in the Circus Maximus. It remained there until 1589

Piazza del Popolo. Emperor Augustus brought the obelisk in the square's centre from Luxor in Egypt when it was placed at the entrance of the city to impress whoever arrived at the city on the Via Flaminia. It must be taken into account that, particularly if we are looking for strange conspiracies and links with the Illuminati, on the date the obelisk is placed in the square, Bernini, the notable master who constantly appears in *Angels and Demons*, had still not been born and that Raphael, the creator of the Chigi Chapel, had already died. In this case, the conspiracy seems to have got in a muddle over timing.

10. PORTA DEL POPOLO

This was originally called the Porta Flaminia, because it was connected to the Via Flaminia, one of the main routes to the old city of Rome and which linked Rome to the Adriatic. It is estimated that this road was built in approximately 220 BC. The name was later changed to Porta del Popolo.

11. THE CHIGI COAT OF ARMS

This is made of curious symbols that appear to imply the union of the powers of heaven and earth. There is a star, perhaps an allusion to the

papacy that one of the family had attained, above some small hills that some have seen as pyramids and that symbolism has been interpreted by experts as the manifestation of the solidity of mountains.

12. HABAKKUK AND THE ANGEL

This statue by Bernini is in the Chigi Chapel. This piece of art is, for many, a warning of the changing times and what is yet to come, and to emphasize this he uses the allegory based on Habakkuk's gift for prophesies.

The story says that Habakkuk was a contemporary of Jeremiah who appears in the Old Testament, although he was less

Habakkuk and the angel, sculpted group by Gianlorenzo Bernini prominent than the other prophet, and little is known about him. In the holy texts, Habakkuk is depicted as a disturbed man, full of doubts about the future of his people and God's kingdom.

In defence of his negativity, Habakkuk makes a prophecy about the invasion of Judea by the Chaldeans and the end of Babylon.

If Bernini's intention was not simply to explain a passage related to the Holy Scriptures, it would be easy to think – like many conspiracy theorists – that Bernini wanted to show in his sculpture the doubts that many were having at that time about the infallibity of the Church.

13. SAINT PETER'S SQUARE

In 1656 Pope Alexander VII chose Bernini as the architect for Saint Peter's Square. Bernini's initial idea was to create a trapezoid surrounded by a two-storey façade but this design was heavily criticized and this is why he decided to build the square the way it is today. Bernini's task was to make a spacious square that would hold multitudes of the faithful.

From a symbolic point of view the square represents the Supreme Pontiff crowned with the tiara, which is represented by the dome of Saint Peter's: his arms are open to welcome all Christians.

14. SAINT PETER'S OBELISK

Erected by the Emperor Augustus in the Foro Juliano, where it stayed for many years until Caligula decided to take to the centre of his own circus, at the foot of Monte Vaticano.

In 1586, Pope Sixtus V decided to position it in front of Saint Peter's Basilica and gave the task to Domenico Fontana. Some years later Bernini was made responsible for designing the elliptic colonnade around the obelisk in the piazza.

The legend states that the original globe at the top of the obelisk contained the ashes of

The obelisk in Saint Peter's Square was a project by the architect Fontana, it was raised in 1586

155

Julius Caesar. However, when refurbishment works took place and the sphere was opened but nothing was found inside. Pope Sixtus V decided to remove the globe from the obelisk and to place a bronze cross that supposedly bears an piece of the true cross, and the Chigi family's coat of arms, in its place. Finally, in 1818, four Egyptian lions were added to the base of the obelisk.

With reference to the Bernini's bas-relief, the large figure seems to symbolize that Bernini wants to strip away with the wind the negative influences still remaining in the area from Roman times. t is worth remembering that the obelisk is located very close to the spot where a Roman circus was held in past times.

The wind seems to express the desire to use the force of the elements (wind is one of the four sacred elements and represents transmutation) to create and to generate new life through the divine breath and to regenerate the air rejecting all things that may harm the establishment.

15. CHURCH OF SANTA MARIA DELLA VICTORIA

This is a Baroque church begun in 1608 by Carlo Maderno. Its most striking interior feature is Bernini's work *The Ecstasy of Saint Teresa*.

16. ECSTASY OF SAINT TERESA

This is a sculpture that Bernini created skilfully between 1647 and 1652. He worked in marble and golden bronze. It is3.5m in height and is kept in the Cornaro Chapel in Santa Maria della Victoria.

Bernini is considered one of the greats in Baroque art and the *Ecstasy of Saint Teresa* is testimony to this. The artist's intention was that the person kneeling at the altar where the sculpture would experience the same mystic state as the saint.

The artist was commissioned to build a chapel in the left side of Santa Maria della Victoria that would be dedicated to Saint Teresa of Avila, founder of the Discalced Carmelite Order.

Bernini started the project and decided to embody the climactic moment when Saint Teresa reaches ecstasy while being visited by an angel holding a burning arrow to penetrate the saint's heart, producing a terrible but simultaneously 'sweet spiritual pain'. This is how the saint would establish direct contact with God.

The saint's expression is dramatically clear: she has reached the greatest and most divine pleasure, ecstasy, but also an erotic kind of

The Ecstasy of Saint Teresa, sculpted by Gianlorenzo Bernini in marble between 1645 and 1652

pleasure, which would be more concrete. This can be seen in the semi-closed eye lids and mouth, and by the tilted face.

Bernini's object seems to be to show delirious mysticism reflected with over-the-top realism and fervour. There is no indication that this work has anything to do with the Iilluminati or any secret society. Nevertheless, it should be pointed out that Bernini wanted to show in his work Saint Teresa reaching a mystic state or one of altered consciousness that leads her to connect, in a full energetic expansion of her whole being, with the angel.

It is also worth stressing that during the 17th century there was a strong focus on the way the arts expressed certain religious events. There were hard times for the Church, which had to fight the divisions Luther was creating. The religious institutions that at other times 'tolerated' certain artistic freedom, now fiercely repressed sculptors and painters who wanted to go further than what was 'politically correct', this is why it is difficult to understand why Bernini was authorized to represent what, for many, was not a mystical allegory but an orgasmic one.

17. PIAZZA NAVONA

Although in the book *Angels and Demons* this square seems linked with water, the truth is that this area has nothing or very little to do with it, with the exception of the fountains. Before the Fountain of the Four Rivers was built in the square, the Circus of Domitian was here.

Fountain of the Four Rivers by Gianlorenzo Bernini. The allegorical figures represent the four continents' largest rivers

18. THE FOUNTAIN OF THE FOUR RIVERS

It was commissioned by Innocent X, through a friend of Bernini, prince Ludovisi. The fountain was started in 1649 and finished in 1651.

In the Piazza Navona was the Palazzo Pamphili with its family chapel devoted to Saint Agnes. The square was somehow a way to show how powerful this family was in Rome. The fountain was simply to furnish the square.

In the fountain Bernini wanted to represent the most important rivers in the four continents: the Danube of Europe, the Rio de la Plata in America, the Nile of Africa and the Indo of Asia. In the same way, the figures that rest on the fountain are symbols of three cultures or worlds: Europe, represented by a horse, Africa, symbolized by a lion, and America, characterized by a cayman.

The fountain is completed by an obelisk upon which a dove sits as an allegory of the Holy Spirit. It was also the emblem of the Pamphili family, which gave them distinction and notable respect from the Church.

19. THE PONTE SANT'ANGELO

This is one of the most exquisite Baroque works. Its creator, Bernini, sculpted ten statues that travel along both sides of the bridge. On this bridge one of the most anticlerical acts in the history of the Church took place. When in 1878, the body of the deceased Pius IX was being

Ponte Sant'Angelo, linking the Vatican with Rome. Bernini sculpted a series of angels with their wings spread as they land on the ground, carrying instruments of the Passion

Photographs of the famous Passeto di Borgo. Thanks to this passage the Pope Nicolas III avoided imprisonment during several attacks

transported along the bridge, a group of agitators tried to throw it into the river Tiber. It is believed that amongst them were many Freemasons trying to start a revolt. According to the chronicles of the time, the Christians who carried the coffin surrounded it to stop it from falling into the river. They resisted the attack and managed to give the Pope a Christian burial.

20. CASTEL SANT'ANGELO

Probably one of the most enigmatic buildings in the Vatican is Castel Sant'Angelo, which has a turbulent history. The first building is dated from AD 139. At the time it must have been Emperor Hadrian's mausoleum. There are many legends explaining his choice; some believe he was advised by Druids who informed him of the strength of the earth's forces in the place. Others say that fortune tellers warned him that it would become famous, and that the Emperor wanted to ensure his name would never be forgotten.

After the Vatican was created, several Popes ordered this building's reconstruction. For centuries it alternated as a prison and a fortress. Today it is a military and artistic museum.

21. THE PASSETO DI BORGO

Also called the 'Corridere del Castel'. Doubtless one of the most curious features of the Vatican is this secret passage connecting the papal apartments with the Castel Sant'Angelo. This passage was built by order of Pope Nicolas III in the 13th century. As with many other European castles it was an escape route. If the Vatican was under attack, the Pope could escape and if discovered he could take refuge in the castle, which was better prepared for defence.

There are innumerable stories regarding this. It has been said that many Popes would use this passage to escape the control of the Vatican and establish secret alliances or liaisons to which it would have been embarassing to admit. It is also thought that some of the Popes who died may have been killed by criminals who used to the passage to reach them.

Bronze angel, statue of the archangel Michael sculpted by the Flemish artist Pieter Verschaffelt

22. THE BRONZE ANGEL

The castle gardens also boast an oddity that has instigated all manner of theories. It is an angel armed with a sword who looks powerfully at visitors from above. What mysteries does this sculpture hide?

In 590, during the Papacy of St Gregory the Great, a plague devastated the city. A procession of penitents was walking around the castle when the Pope had a vision: he saw an angel with an unsheathed sword flying overhead. The Pontiff believed that this was God's response to his prayers to stop the plague and declared that it had ended. The next day there were no more cases of plague, and as a sign of gratitude, the Pope ordered this sculpture to be built.

BERNINI: ARTIST OR CONSPIRATOR

This appendix would be incomplete without the inclusion of one of the figures most linked (even if it is through art) to *Angels and Demons*. It is difficult to know if Bernini belonged to a secret society associated to the Illuminati. If we take into account the close relationship between the artist and the Church it seems quite improbable. Nevertheless, one should always leave room for doubt. It may be that Bernini did not directly operate through his work with symbols that would serve as a secret guide to others, but what if his assistants did? We know that artists did not work alone. To do so would have meant a very limited production.

Bernini, like many other geniuses such as Raphael, Leonardo or even Michelangelo, could have not been everywhere at once. He had to delegate. He gave precise instructions carried out by others on his behalf. Bernini was hard-working but he was not omnipresent. He supervized and took credit for the work but it would have been impossible for him to complete all his commissions himself. Maybe, and only maybe, he was an innocent artist, and others incorporated minute details to communicate their secret.

Gianlorenzo Bernini (b. Naples, 1598, d. Rome, 1680) was the exceptional figure of the classic Roman Baroque. Son of the sculptor Pietro Bernini, his family moved to Rome in 1604. He was already a renowned sculptor at the age of 20 and started out as an architect when Maffeo Barberini Pope Urban VIII in 1624. A mere five years later he was awarded the job of architect for the Saint Peter's. The majority of his best-known structures belong to his later years, mainly during the Papacy of Alexander VII Chigi (1655–1667). Bernini helped to change the face of Rome. He renewed many stylistic concepts, above all in the way in which he played with space and with his talent for achieving optical and lighting effects, to creat false perspective.

Giovani Lorenzo Bernini,
the artist who contributed
towards changing the
landscape of Rome

BEYOND
ANGELS
AND
DEMONS

GLOSSARY

GLOSSARY

TRUTH BEHIND FICTION
(CHARACTERS, PLACES AND OTHER TERMS)

AMBIGRAM: Texts made up of one or more words that can be read in the same way when rotated through 180 degrees.

Ambigrams are mystical initiation texts transmitting magical sensations. They are not part of a secret code as they are normally easy to read. The object is the meditative abstraction of the reader.

GIANLORENZO BERNINI: One of the geniuses of the Italian Baroque (Naples, 1598-Rome, 1680). There are no records of any links with secret societies, and a link with the Illuminati is even less likely as the sect was created eighty years after his death.

CAMERLENGO: President of the Apostolic Chamber and responsible for preparing for and managing the Conclave's activities.

Tradition dictates that upon finding the Supreme Pontiff dead, he must call his name three times. If there is no answer, following the correct procedures he will recognize that the Pope has died and announce it formally in order to start the Conclave.

CERN (CONSEIL EUROPEEN POUR LA RECHERCHE NUCLEAIRE): Founded in Geneva in 1978. There are no records of an X-33 aircraft belonging to this organization. What we know today as the internet was invented within the institution.

CERN has a particle accelerator. The first collision between matter and antimatter was achieved there in 1981, leading to the discovery that the energy released could exceed nuclear fission 1,000-fold.

CICERONE: the person with the task of explaining the peculiarities of a city, building or institution.

CONCLAVE: the name of the ceremony and ritual of choosing a new . Pope. Members of the College of Cardinals lock themselves away from the world until they agree upon a suitable Supreme Pontiff.

The protocol of the Conclave follows the last wishes of the pope stated in a constitutional document of succession.

DIALOGA, DISCORSI, DIAGRAMMA: Supposedly the name of three pieces of work by Galileo Galilei. The reality is that Galileo began writing the *Dialogue on the Tides* in 1624. In 1630 the Church censors accepted the text but changed its title to *Dialogue on the Two Great World Systems*; it was published in 1632. Subsequent to the trial against Galileo and his later recantation, all copies of the *Dialogue* were burnt by explicit order of the Inquisition.

Galileo's *Discorsi* is really a number of written pieces and texts by the scientist that discuss physics and mathematical principles.
There is no record of the piece *Diagramma*, which could actually be any of his scientific drawings.

THE FOUR ELEMENTS: According to ancient science these are water, earth, air and fire. Some have considered the existence of a fifth element, which they call ether.

These four elements are archetypes of physical and emotional states. Water represents the capacity of metamorphosis because it can go from being solid, to gaseous and finally liquid. Air symbolizes the capacity of adaptation and ideas. Earth is continuity, steadfastness and resistance. Finally, fire is linked to revolution, change, strength and the aggressive transformation of things that are theoretically unalterable.

GALILEO GALILEI: Italian physicist and astronomer. He was born in 1564 and died in 1642. Together with Johannes Kepler he began a scientific revolution that overthrew the beliefs of the time. He was not an Illuminati member as the order had still not been created but he could have had contact with the esoteric and philosophical world of the Rosicrucians.

His scientific discoveries led him to confrontations with the Church. In 1633 he was judged and forced to renounce officially all his theories that the Earth was not the centre of the world and orbited around the Sun.

GAIA: Mother Earth. The theorists who believe the Earth is a living and intelligent entity call it Gaia or Gaya. One of the great defendants of this theory is the scientist Rupert Sheldrake.

GREAT ELECTOR: Member of the Curia and the equal in rank to the camerlengo. It is the name given to the Master of Ceremonies of the Conclave, who has the mission of ensuring a smooth-running voting procedure.

HASH-ASHIN: Sect of mercenary warriors founded in the 11th century by

Hassan-Ben-Sabbah. They reach an altered state of consciousness through the ritual ingestion of hashish. They were extremely cruel.

HATHA YOGA: In Sanskrit the word 'yoga' means 'tie'. The objective of yoga is the physical and mental control of the body. There are many types, Hatha yoga is the physical kind that cleanses the body and maintains fitness. It is the best-known form of yoga and also has the most complicated physical disciplines.

ILLUMINATI: Name by which the Illuminati of Bavaria are known.

ILLUMINATI OF BAVARIA: Secret and conspiratorial group created by Adam Weishaupt in 1776. The order was officially disbanded ten years later.

LINGUA PURA: Colloquial name of the language adopted by the scientists of Galileo's time. It is unlikely that this 'lingua' was English as they all spoke Latin or Italian.

LUCIFER: Name of the fallen angel who broke away from God after confronting Him. He was the leader of the rebel angels who sought knowledge. Poetically he is the morning star, the first light to show the way. The followers of Lucifer's doctrine are called Luciferians.

MASONRY: (Popularly known as Freemasonry) Brought about by the first groups of builders and master builders who constructed the Gothic cathedrals. Although Masonry declares that its origins lie in pharonic Egypt, modern Masonry was founded in 1717, the year in which the Great Lodge of England was formed; the French version was established in 1732.

NOVO ORDO SECULORUM: Terminology for the new secular order linked in modern times to the new world order. This term appears in Latin on the US dollar and the English concept was introduced by George Bush at the end of the 20th century.

PHYSICS: in *Angels and Demons* there are many terms related to this area of science. The most relevant are:

> **ANTIMATTER**: matter composed from antiparticles or matter in which every particle has been substituted by an antiparticle.

> **ATOM**: the smallest particle of a body that can be altered through

a chemical reaction.

ELECTRON: a light elemental particle that forms part of an atom. It ontains the lowest possible negative electrical charge.

KILOTON: a unit used only in military terms to establish the power of nuclear weapons. A kiloton has the same explosive power as a 1,000 ton TNT bomb. The bombs used during the Second World War were 20 kilotons. Nuclear bombs are measured in megatons, and a megaton equals a million tons of TNT.

PROTON: Elemental particle that is on its own the nucleus of the hydrogen atom.

TRINACRIA: Instead of being the symbol of an eye inside a triangle, it is a face with wings and three legs, one protruding from the top of the head and the other two from what would be the shoulders.
It is the old symbol of the Island of Trinacria, now called Sicily.

X-33: The name of a project for a spaceship, which has yet to see the light of day. Tests were officially abandoned in November 1999.

YIN YANG: A Chinese philosophical concept of opposite forces that complement each other. Yin is associated with darkness, moisture, passiveness and the feminine, and yang represents brightness, dryness, energy and the masculine.

ROME: PLACES AND BUILDINGS

ANGEL OF CASTEL SANT'ANGELO: A bronze figure that Pope Gregory the Great had erected in 590. Located at the highest point in the gardens of the Castel Sant'Angelo.

DEMON'S HOLE: The oculus of the Pantheon. It has a diameter of 43.2 metres.

CHIGI CHAPEL: Inside the Church of Santa Maria del Popolo. It belonged to one of the richest families in Rome.

CASTEL SANT'ANGELO: Linked to the Vatican through the Passetto. Dates from 139 or earlier.

FOUNTAIN OF THE FOUR RIVERS: Erected by Bernini following Innocent X's commission. The fountain depicts the most significant rivers in the world known at the time. It also has an obelisk crowned with a dove.

OBELISK OF THE PIAZZA DEL POPOLO: Ramses II ordered its construction. It comes from Luxor and is the tallest in Rome. It is opposite the gate that give access to the old Via Flaminia.

PANTHEON: Roman temple dedicated to the planet's seven most significant deities. Also known as Agrippa's Pantheon.

PIAZZA NAVONA: Contains Bernini's Fountain of the Four Rivers.

PIAZZA DEL POPOLO: Contains the Church of Santa Maria del Popolo and the tallest obelisk in Rome.

PONTE SANT'ANGELO: By Bernini, who incorporated ten statues of angels on the bridge.

PORTA DEL POPOLO: Once one of the main entrances to the city of Rome. It faces the obelisk of the same name.

SANTA MARIA DELLA VITTORIA: Houses Bernini's *The Ecstasy of Saint Teresa*.

SANTA MARIA DEL POPOLO: Basilica begun in 1099, next to the ancient walls of Rome. It is in the Piazza del Popolo.

RAPHAEL'S TOMB: Found inside the Pantheon.

VATICAN: PLACES AND BUILDINGS

PASSETO DEL BORGO: A secret corridor linking the pope's chambers to the Castel Sant'Angelo. It was built by Pope Nicolas in the 13th century.

SAINT PETER'S BASILICA: Supposed to have been built over the tomb of the Apostle which is at the high altar, the centre of the basilica.

SAINT PETER'S SQUARE: Designed by Bernini under the patronage of Pope Alexander VI. It represents the Supreme Pontiff crowned with the tiara on Saint Peter's Dome, his arms are open to embrace the faithful.

The obelisk of Saint Peter is in the piazza and it is surrounded by an elliptical colonnade also designed by Bernini.

SISTINE CHAPEL: Commissioned by Pope Sixtus VI, with frescoes by the greatest Renaissance artists. It is where the members of the College of Cardinals meet.

SECRET ARCHIVES OF THE VATICAN: Next to the Vatican Library. It was built in the 17th century on the orders of Pope Paul V. It houses all documents related to pastoral activities and the actions of the Vatican government. The Secret Archives can be visited from 16 September to 15 July every year, upon application to the prefect.